Modeling TANKS and MILITARY VEHICLES

BY SHEPERD PAINE

SCALE MODELING HANDBOOK No.6

All photographs and models by the author unless otherwise credited

Editor: Bob Hayden   Art Director: Lawrence Luser
Copy Editor: Burr Angle   Staff Artist: Bill Scholz
Editorial Assistant: Marcia Stern   Assistant Copy Editor: Rich Bowen
Editorial Secretary: Monica Borowicki

First printing, 1982. Second printing, 1983. Third printing, 1987. Fourth printing, 1989. Fifth printing, 1990. Sixth printing, 1993.

KALMBACH BOOKS

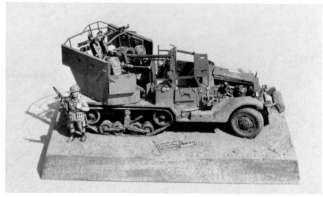

Armor modeling runs the gamut — from a fairly stock version of a 1/35 scale kit such as the Tamiya Bren carrier by Francois Verlinden (left), to superbly detailed conversions like Steve Zaloga's 1/76 scale M15A1 gun motor carriage (above). The conversion, believe it or not, was based on a Matchbox M16 kit.

Foreword

Tanks and armored vehicles have been popular subjects for plastic modelers almost as long as plastic kits have existed. The first armor kits appeared in the U. S. during the late '50s, and a brief but active flurry of activity among such makers as Revell, Adams ("SNAP"), Renwal, and Monogram followed. Several of those early kits remain on the market today, often under different brand names, and a few still compare favorably in quality with more recent offerings.

In the early years the popularity of armor modeling seemed to run in cycles. After the initial surge of kit releases, armor models practically disappeared from hobbyshop shelves until a

trickle of new kits from Japan in the late '60s triggered a resurgence of interest. Today, we armor modelers are blessed with an abundance of precisely detailed kits beyond the wildest dreams of the struggling enthusiasts of those lean years, who had to wrestle with clunky clockwork motors and rubber-band tracks.

Much of the current popularity of armored vehicle models results from the widespread interest in almost every aspect of World War II that has developed during the last 15 years. The volume of printed material generated to satisfy that interest has triggered a parallel interest in modeling; indeed, the modeling activity may well be a di-

rect result of the wealth of available research material. While modelers today take for granted the wealth of pictorial information at their fingertips (whole books can be found on one particular type of vehicle), only a few years ago the total number of books about armor could have been counted on the fingers of one hand.

So, if you are just starting out in armor modeling, you've come in at just the right time. And, if you've been an armor modeler for a few years, count your blessings — the pickings were not always this rich!

Armor modeling scales. Armored vehicle models have always come in a bewildering variety of scales. The very first armor kits were often scaled simply to fit in a particular size box and seldom advertised a scale at all. Still, early Revell and Adams kits generally measured out to 1/40 scale, Renwal to 1/32, and Monogram to 1/35. The development of 1/35 scale to its present dominance is an interesting story. While it is true that this scale was made popular by the Japanese manufacturers during their takeover of the market in the 1960s, I suspect they chose 1/35 scale because most of their early offerings were based on the earlier American kits, particularly the Monogram 1/35 series. As the Japanese makers began to introduce new kits of their own they simply adopted the same scale for convenience and continuity.

The smaller armor scales have origins in model railroading. When Roco

Many armor modeling techniques apply just as well to many other kinds of models. Jim Stephens, whose tanks are featured throughout this book, made full use of the modeling and weathering methods he developed for his armor models when he built this heavily converted 1/25 scale model of the tank truck from the movie "Duel."

first introduced their Minitanks series in the early '60s, they used 1/87 or HO scale. Airfix, who brought out their first armor kits at about the same time, opted for 1/76 — British model railroad OO scale. Both these sizes remain popular today.

Some manufacturers have tried brief flirtations with 1/48 scale (model railroad O scale and a popular size for model aircraft) and 1/24 scale for armor, but there have been no new releases in these sizes for some time, so they may prove to have been flashes in the pan. Most armor modelers tend to stick to one scale for the bulk of their collection, but there is no compelling reason to do so. You may find that you feel more comfortable working in one scale than another, but there is nothing that says you can't play the field a bit, either.

Although this book covers armor modeling in all scales, I think it's appropriate that I concentrate on 1/35, since this is by far the most popular size among serious armor modelers. Modeling techniques, however, don't vary significantly from one scale to the next, and in the rare instances that they do, I'll take pains to point out how.

We'll start at the beginning. Even if you have no experience in plastic modeling at all, don't worry — we'll start at the bottom and work our way up. In fact, armor modeling is the ideal field for beginning modelers, far better than cars or airplanes. No other modeling category is more forgiving of mistakes, and in no other field can a novice turn out as respectable an effort the first time out. The reason for this lies in the nature of the armor models and kits themselves. While they may have more pieces than other kits, armor models have very few seams to fill, sand, or file, and in general, a degree of grubbiness in the finished model is actually a virtue, not a fault.

Once you've built two or three kits using the techniques explained in the early chapters of this book, you'll find that you'll be able to advance your skills quickly, first learning how to modify stock kits, and eventually moving on to major conversions and even scratchbuilt models. And what's more, armor modeling is fun!

The parts of a tank. Armored fighting vehicles have their own special jargon, like any branch of the service, and though I'll have to refer readers to reference books for in-depth glossaries, beginning modelers should study the accompanying illustrations to learn the basic nomenclature you'll need to understand this book. Then, on to Chapter 1!

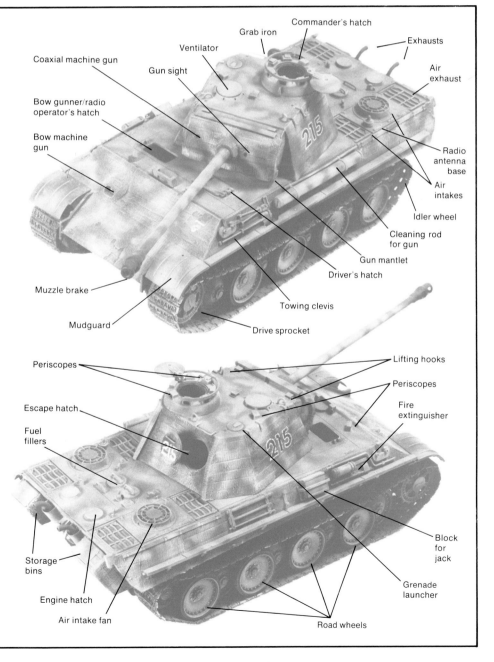

PARTS OF A TANK

The first British tanks in WWI were developed under the auspices of the Royal Navy, so many armor terms have a distinctly nautical flavor.

Drive sprocket: Connected to the engine by the transmission and drive train, this wheel makes the track go around. The sprocket on each side can be driven independently, causing the vehicle to turn. On modern tanks the drive sprocket is often mounted at the rear instead of the front.

Idler: A free-turning wheel at the back or front of the suspension. The idler can be moved forward or back to adjust track tension.

Road wheels: These free-turning wheels on heavily sprung axles form the most important element of the suspension. They allow the vehicle to move smoothly over rough terrain. **Return rollers** (not shown) are small wheels that carry the track above the road wheels as it returns from the idler to the drive sprocket.

Towing clevis: Part of the gear used to rig the tank for towing or retrieval.

Muzzle brake: This device reduces the recoil of the gun and directs most of the blast to the sides, reducing the amount of dust kicked up (which would obscure the gunner's vision for the next shot).

Gun mantlet: The heavily armored, movable gun shield, usually removable with the gun as part of a single assembly.

Coaxial machine gun: Mounted parallel to the main gun, this is used as an antipersonnel weapon and occasionally as a "spotter" (one quick burst of tracers to make sure the gun is on target, followed immediately by a round from the main gun).

Lifting hooks: Used to remove the turret for maintenance.

Escape hatch: Usually found on the back, bottom, or side of the tank, this small hatch allows the crew to escape under fire in an emergency.

Grenade launcher: A very short range mortar used to lob antipersonnel grenades at attacking infantry.

Grab iron — Commander's hatch — Exhausts — Air exhaust — Ventilator — Coaxial machine gun — Gun sight — Bow gunner/radio operator's hatch — Bow machine gun — Radio antenna base — Air intakes — Idler wheel — Cleaning rod for gun — Gun mantlet — Driver's hatch — Muzzle brake — Towing clevis — Mudguard — Drive sprocket

Periscopes — Lifting hooks — Periscopes — Escape hatch — Fuel fillers — Fire extinguisher — Storage bins — Block for jack — Engine hatch — Grenade launcher — Air intake fan — Road wheels

The Italeri 1/35 scale M7 "Priest" self-propelled howitzer is a good kit for a beginner to start with.

1
Basic kit assembly

If you already have some experience in building plastic kits, reading this chapter will serve as a quick review of what you already know and may even introduce a few things you don't. If you've had little or no experience with plastic kits, this chapter will ensure that you start out right.

Choosing your first armor kit. If we take the idea of starting at the beginning literally, that means opening our discussion with the purchase of your first kit. Because some kits go together much easier than others, making a poor selection can make building your first model harder than it has to be. Even if you have decided on a particular scale, the range of choices is rather wide — sometimes, even slightly bewildering.

My advice: First, start with a kit offered by a major manufacturer, one who has an extensive line of armor kits (usually, you can count on experienced manufacturers to make kits that fit together well). Second, don't let

the number of parts in the box influence your decision, because all armor kits, by their very nature, contain lots of parts. Third, don't worry about accuracy or authenticity. Some kits are inaccurate, but this should not be a consideration in choosing the first few you build. Later, as you gain experience and knowledge, authenticity will become an increasingly important factor in your choices.

Finally, be aware that many excellent older kits incorporate shortcuts in design and tooling that were acceptable when the kits were introduced, but that are looked upon with horror in the more sophisticated market of today. The best example of this is shovels and other tools molded directly on the tank hull rather than supplied as separate parts.

How do you find out all these things before you buy a kit? Ask the clerk. Clerks in hobby shops are often quite knowledgeable modelers themselves, and they can be a big help to you. Even

if the clerk doesn't build armor models, he probably has heard feedback about various kits from customers. It pays to ask for advice.

Tools and materials. Once you have a kit, the next thing you'll need is a place to work. This needn't be fancy or permanent — some very fine models have been built on the kitchen table. All you really need is a flat surface, a comfortable chair, and adequate light. Strangely enough, in many ways the floor is a more important consideration than the table. If the floor is the same basic color as your model, or multicolored, or textured, you can anticipate spending a certain amount of time on your hands and knees searching for dropped parts. I once tried to work in a room with a shag carpet; the experiment was an absolute disaster — anything that dropped off the work surface simply vanished forever!

You'll need the following basic modeling tools:

• Hobby knife — X-acto is the most

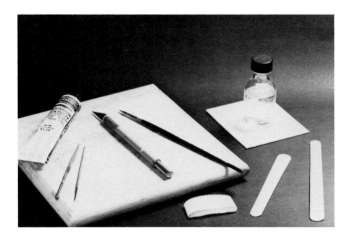

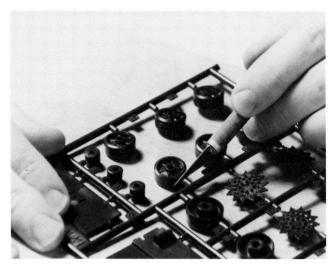

Basic tools and materials for kit assembly. From left: plastic body putty ("green stuff"), needle files, hobby knife, loop of masking tape for small parts, cement brush, liquid cement bottle epoxied to piece of card, and emery boards for sanding.

Always cut parts from their molding sprues with a knife.

common brand found in hobby shops, and the No. 11 blade is the most useful shape. The blades dull quickly, so buy two or three packages of extra blades, and don't hesitate to replace them.

• Sandpaper — Extra fine, fine, and medium grits. Emery boards (intended for shaping fingernails) are readily available in drugstores and are ideal for modelwork.

• Liquid plastic cement — Most plastic cements are solvents that dissolve mating plastic surfaces, forming a weld-like bond. Liquid plastic cements are neater and easier to work with than those that come in a tube.

• Plastic filler putty — This is used for filling gaps to make a smooth surface. Absolutely essential for aircraft models, it isn't needed as often for armor models. Still, a tube of filler is an essential item in your tool kit.

• Optional equipment — These items aren't absolutely essential, but they can make your modeling easier: A cutting board (standard kitchen variety) to avoid scarring your work table; small needle files (round, square, and triangular), which are neater and more precise for certain jobs than sandpaper; spring clamps and rubber bands to hold parts together while cementing — not needed often for armor models, but useful; and masking tape, which, when formed in a loop and stuck to the cut-

ting board sticky side out, makes a handy parking place for small parts during assembly and painting.

Getting ready to work. The great bugaboo of building kits is losing parts. Even if you faithfully follow the dictum of never cutting a part from its molding tree until you are ready to use it, parts get knocked off the trees during shipment, or roll onto the floor when you aren't looking. I've never found a way to eliminate this problem altogether, but you can minimize it by taking a few minutes to organize your work area. Keep your work area clear and uncluttered so you can find things easily, and have a small, shallow box handy to store all loose parts until they are called for.

The worst disaster that can befall your model is to spill a bottle of liquid cement on it. The cement ruins the parts, and in many cases the kit is a total loss. This calamity can be avoided easily, however, by making your cement spill-proof. Glue the bottle to a piece of wood, plastic, or cardboard with 5-minute epoxy, or simply embed it in a large blob of modeling clay. Drill a hole in a block of wood if you are ambitious, or quickly cut a hole in a piece of foam rubber with a pair of scissors. Just make sure there is no way your cement bottle can accidentally overturn.

Now you're finally ready to open the box. Resist the urge to greedily fondle the parts, and remove only the instruction sheet. Read through it carefully, noting the order in which the parts are to be assembled. Look for complex assemblies where the order of assembling the parts is critical, and make notes on the instructions to remind yourself to take extra care with them. Few things are more frustrating than finding a part left over and discovering that the place where it belongs is no longer accessible.

Next open the parts bag and carefully remove the trees on which the parts are molded (these are called "sprues," and I'll use that term from now on). Check to see if any parts have broken loose, and try to identify where they fit in the sprue. If the instructions include a parts layout diagram, check each sprue against it; if any parts are missing or deformed, now is the time to find out. Do not remove any part from its sprue until it is required for assembly.

Preparing parts for assembly. As each part is called for by the kit instructions, carefully cut it from its sprue with your modeling knife. Never twist parts off the sprues — doing so leaves an indented scar in the part that cannot be trimmed off.

Examine each part for lines left on it

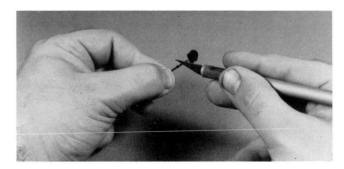

To remove molding lines, use a backward, scraping motion of the hobby knife, holding the blade perpendicular to the surface.

A scrap of fine steel wool works well for removing sanding scratches and file marks and smoothing joints between parts.

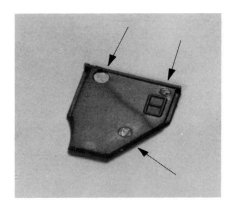

Raised knockout pin marks left during manufacturing can be shaved away with a knife, but more often the marks are depressions, which must be filled with putty and sanded flush after the putty has dried.

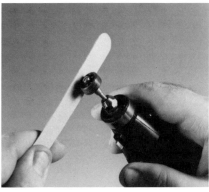

Trimming parting lines from wheels with a knife can be tedious. If you have a motor tool, you can speed up the job by mounting each wheel in the tool and rotating it at slow speed against an emery board.

A round needle file is useful for smoothing inside the road wheel hubs. Preparing wheels is tedious, so I get it out of the way as soon as possible, keeping the wheels in a small box so none get lost.

where the halves of the mold meet. Carefully shave away these molding lines (also called "parting lines") in any location where they will be visible on the finished model. I consider this one of the most tedious aspects of armor modeling (because there are so many parts), but it simply must be done. Absence of molding lines is one of the things that clearly distinguishes the work of an experienced modeler from that of a beginner — an experienced modeler never leaves visible molding lines.

A backward scraping motion with the knife is most effective for removing molding lines. If you try to slice the molding lines away by pushing the knife blade into the plastic, the blade will tend to dig in, leaving irregular gouges in the surface of the part.

Also watch for circular marks on the surface of the parts. These "knockout marks" are made by the rods which eject the parts from the mold during manufacturing, and like the molding lines, they must be carefully scraped away. If the knockout marks are recessed, you'll have to fill them with plastic putty and sand the surface smooth.

The neatest and most efficient way to use liquid plastic cement is to assemble the parts and then gently touch a brush full of cement to the top of seam.

Today, manufacturers try to locate knockout marks on the unseen side of the part, where you won't have to bother with them, but this is not always possible. In recent kits the manufacturers make the knockout rods push against small plastic tabs projecting from the sides of some of the parts; the tabs are easily removed.

Some of the most tedious parts to clean in armor kits are the road wheels. A small hand power tool helps here: Attach the wheel to the tool arbor, chuck the wheel and arbor in the tool, set the speed control on low, and smooth the rim of the spinning wheel with an emery board. To prevent friction-generated heat from melting the wheel, run the tool on low speed and use only light sanding pressure.

Using liquid cement. There are several tricks to using liquid plastic cement. First, don't try to use the applicator brush provided in the cap; it is far too coarse for fine modelwork. Instead, use a medium-quality No. 0 watercolor brush, perhaps an old brush that's past its prime. Mark this brush in some way (wrapping masking tape around the handle works fine) and use it only for cementing.

Although the old "brush cement on one part, brush it on the other, and stick 'em together" routine will work well for small parts, for larger ones the solvent cement evaporates too quickly for this method to be effective. In those cases, it is better to fit the two parts together dry, then touch a brush full of cement lightly to the top of the seam. The cement will flow into the gap between the parts, where gravity and capillary action will carry it all the way down to the end, forming a strong, neat joint. Be careful to keep your fingers away from the seam, or capillary action will also carry the solvent under your fingers, ruining the surface of the model.

Armor models rarely call for clamping of any kind, but gluing clamps are preferable to rubber bands as holding

devices during assembly, because capillary action can carry the solvent along the rubber band and across the surface of the model. If you must use a rubber band, place small wood spacer blocks between it and the model to keep the rubber band away from the seam.

Test fitting and assembly. Always test the fit of parts before assembling them with cement. You may have misunderstood the instructions, or some parting lines may require additional smoothing for a proper fit. Occasionally, the manufacturer makes a mistake, and you'll have to trim a part slightly to allow a perfect fit.

Some parts shouldn't be cemented at all. For instance, when installing road wheels and running gear, leave all the wheels turnable. This makes track installation easier, but more important, greatly facilitates painting the rubber tires on the wheels later on.

Filling seams. One advantage of modeling armor is that most of the joints between parts in armor kits occur in the same places as seams on the real thing, thereby creating natural-looking joints that require no filling, sanding, or filing. (If you've built a few aircraft kits, you know what a blessing this is.) The most notable exception is tank gun barrels, which often come molded in two parts. Because the gun is one of the most prominent features of a tank, care should be taken to smooth over this seam completely.

The easiest way to make smooth, invisible seams between parts is to apply a bit more cement to the joint than usual, giving the cement a few extra seconds to dissolve the plastic before joining the parts. Squeeze the parts together tightly, until a bead of softened plastic appears along the seam, then set the piece aside to dry overnight. The next day, go back and scrape off the bead with your knife; this should leave a smooth, invisible seam. If there are flaws, use liquid cement, acetone, or lacquer thinner to thin a small

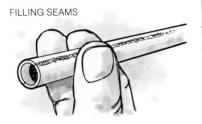

When assembling, use a liberal amount of cement, and squeeze the joint hard, until a bead of molten plastic appears along the seam.

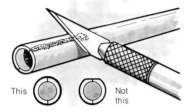

This   Not this

When the bead is thoroughly dry, shave it down carefully with a knife, taking care not to flatten round contours.

If the seam still shows, apply filler putty and smooth with a brush and acetone or lacquer thinner. When dry, sand and steel wool the putty smooth, again being careful not to flatten curved contours.

This is the Italeri M7 Priest hull and gun subassembly before installing the sides.

The M7 suspension is fully operational. Instead of gluing it together, it should be assembled so the wheels rotate and the arms swivel. This is not so you can play with your model on the rug, but so that you have the option of showing off the articulated suspension on a landscaped base.

After installing the sides the seams must be eliminated. This can sometimes be done simply by scraping after the cement has dried, but usually you'll have to use plastic body putty. Take care with this step; seams that are visible but shouldn't be are a sure sign of a careless modeler.

amount of body putty to the consistency of honey and brush it onto the seam, smoothing it over with a brush moistened with the same solvent. After the filler putty dries thoroughly, sand with fine sandpaper, then rub the area down with fine steel wool.

When to paint. When you first examine the kit instructions make a note of which parts must be painted; if you like, circle them. In general, you can ignore the manufacturer's recommendations to paint small parts on the sprues, because they would only have to be touched up later. In fact, on armor models it's usually easier to paint such parts in place, after the model has been assembled.

Nevertheless, certain parts must be painted before installation; whenever possible, set these aside to be painted and added after the rest of the model is painted. I suggest you consider painting during assembly only as a last resort. Armor modeling is a lot easier when you can spray the whole model with a basic overall color without worrying about painting over previously painted details.

Working with subassemblies. Subassemblies are logical sections of a model that may themselves consist of many parts, such as the cannon and mount of a self-propelled gun. Often you will want to keep certain sub-

assemblies separate from the rest of the model until you have had a chance to paint around, underneath, or inside them. For example, I never glue a tank turret into place until all painting and weathering have been completed.

Try to train yourself to identify logical subassemblies that will help simplify construction and painting. This kind of thinking calls for both forethought and continued planning as you work. Eventually, you'll encounter unusual cases such as leaving the whole top section of the hull loose to facilitate painting those parts of the interior that will be visible through open hatches. The best general rule with subassemblies is "when in doubt, leave it loose," because it is easier to go back and cement a few things that could have been attached earlier than it is to pry loose something that should not have been attached at all.

Tracks and track tension. In most armor kits, the tracks are made of a flexible, rubbery plastic such as vinyl.

Since plastic cements and most glues won't bond the tracks, they usually have to be assembled using heat. The most efficient tool for this operation is a small soldering iron, but a small

Work in subassemblies whenever you can. This is the completed 105 mm gun.

To assemble tracks with a soldering iron don't actually touch the rubber with the tip of the iron, just let the radiant heat mushroom the heads of the rubber pins. Tap the pins flat with your finger while they are still hot to make the joint less visible.

Track that is too loose or too tight can be adjusted by moving the idler wheel back or forward. Since this involves breaking the wheel off and gluing it back, it is a last resort, but it does work and is a good deal better than tracks that don't fit.

screwdriver heated over a candle or cigarette lighter (or a match, if you're desperate) will also do nicely.

To assemble the tracks, carefully align the track ends, holding them in place with one hand while touching the soldering iron or heated screwdriver blade to the joining pins with your other hand. Don't go overboard; just enough heat to mushroom the pins and make a secure bond is all that's needed — too much heat will turn the track into a gooey mess. To make the joint almost invisible, gently flatten the mushroomed heads with your finger while they are still hot.

Snap the assembled tracks onto the model to test the fit. The fit should be tight enough that there is no slack, but not so tight that the tracks bow inward where they pass over the drive sprockets.

Here a word about tracks on real armored vehicles is in order. Track tension is a critical factor: Tracks that are too tight will snap under strain, tracks that are too loose run the risk of slipping off the drive sprocket. On most vehicles track tension is adjusted by moving the idler wheel forward or back.

Optimum track tension varies from one vehicle to the next. On tanks with return rollers, such as the Sherman and Panzer IV, the tracks should be tight, with no visible slack. (This was actually the case on Shermans, but most photos of Panzer IVs show a little slack between the return rollers.) On vehicles with high drive sprockets and no return rollers, such as the German Tiger and Panther, most Russian tanks, and the U. S. M113 personnel carrier, a certain degree of slack is desirable, and the correct tension is determined by measuring the distance between the returning track and the top of one of the road wheels.

Modeling track tension realistically is often a problem, mainly because the rubber tracks provided in the kits don't always want to behave like the real ones. Tight tracks are easiest to model; if the kit is properly engineered the fit should be perfect. If the tracks are noticeably too loose or too tight, correct the tension in the same way as on the real vehicle — move the idler wheel forward or back. This means breaking the idler off, since by the time you fit the tracks it has been permanently installed on the model. When you reposition the idler on the model, use a generous amount of plastic cement and be sure to let the joint set for at least 24 hours before you reinstall the track, so the bond has a chance to develop maximum strength.

A graceful sag is important to the realism of loose-tracked vehicles, and there are several ways to achieve it. The simplest is to tie the track to the road wheel axle below it with black thread. The thread can be pulled down tight, or loosened slightly to give a gentle curve to the slack. It may take two or more such ties to get the right appearance.

In some cases, such as the slight sag in the track between the return rollers on a Panzer IV, the tie method cannot be used because there is no way to conceal the thread. Here, the solution is to

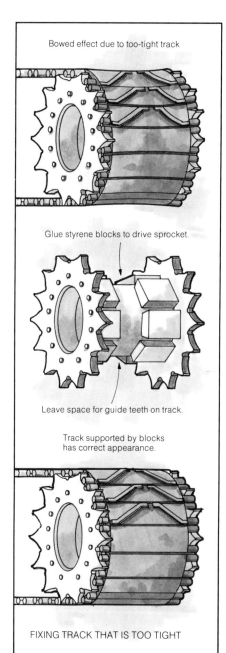

Bowed effect due to too-tight track

Glue styrene blocks to drive sprocket.

Leave space for guide teeth on track.

Track supported by blocks has correct appearance.

FIXING TRACK THAT IS TOO TIGHT

Although the technical specifications usually call for tracks on vehicles with return rollers to be kept tight, tanks in the field often have a certain amount of slack, particularly those with metal tracks. Model and photo by Belgian modeler Francois Verlinden.

drill holes through the hull and insert straight pins to force the track down from above. Small blocks of styrene on the inside of the hull will keep the pins from gradually tilting upward due to the constant pressure from the track.

Minor kit modifications. Although this chapter is limited to assembling kits straight from the box, there are a number of minor standard modifications that are simply the mark of a careful modeler. The most common is to drill out the ends of small caliber cannons and machine guns. You don't even need a drill for this: Touch the point of a sharp modeling knife to the center of the barrel end and slowly twist it. As the point works into the barrel twist more vigorously until a hole of the desired diameter is obtained. Pay less attention to the depth (a drop of black paint will give it plenty), but concentrate instead on keeping the hole centered.

Another minor modification is to replace delicate plastic grab handles with sturdy ones made of brass wire. Soft brass wire, available at hobby and craft stores, is easily formed with needle-nose pliers and can be glued in place with super glue.

Also easy and worthwhile is to replace the cast-plastic tow cables with more realistic ones of twisted solder wire (see Chapter 5) or picture hanging cord (some types of string also work well). Cut off the tow cable ends, drill them out slightly with your knife, and glue them to the ends of the new cable, which can either be stowed in the regulation fashion or simply looped haphazardly over the vehicle.

The final check. After your model is completely assembled check the parts sprues for anything you might have overlooked. Even experienced modelers sometimes find something they can't remember ever having seen before and then have to search through the instructions to figure out what it is and where it goes!

Next, check the model over carefully, looking for molding lines you forgot to clean, knockout pin circles, seams that ought to be filled, or spots of cement that will mar the appearance of the finished model. The cement stains can be carefully scraped smooth with a knife, but only after they have been allowed to set overnight and the dissolved plastic has re-hardened.

Incidentally, if you spill cement on the surface of the model don't try to wipe it off — doing so will only turn a minor disaster into a major one. Just blow vigorously on the cement spill, spreading it across as much of the surface as possible so it will evaporate quickly and do less damage.

After you've inspected it thoroughly and corrected all flaws, your model is ready for painting, which is the subject of our next chapter.

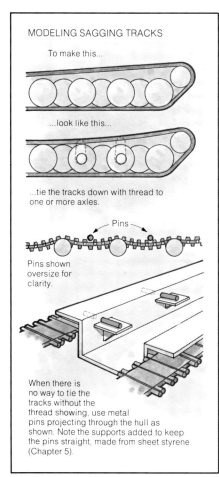

MODELING SAGGING TRACKS

To make this...

...look like this...

...tie the tracks down with thread to one or more axles.

Pins —

Pins shown oversize for clarity.

When there is no way to tie the tracks without the thread showing, use metal pins projecting through the hull as shown. Note the supports added to keep the pins straight, made from sheet styrene (Chapter 5).

An important extra modeling touch, even for your first kit, is to hollow out the ends of all gun barrels. This is easily done by twisting a hole with the point of a sharp hobby knife (above), or by drilling with a pin vise and drill bit (below).

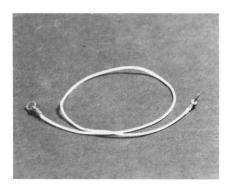

The all-plastic tow cables provided in kits are often poorly molded, and should be replaced with string or wire picture cord. Simply cut off the molded cable end fittings, hollow out the ends a bit with your knife, and glue the fittings to the ends of a length of string or braided wire.

The assembled Italeri M7 Priest kit. A few minor scratches still have to be removed with fine steel wool, but other than that the model is ready for painting.

One great advantage of armor models is that most can be painted after assembly, which greatly simplifies finishing.

2
Painting armor models

The first rule of serious modeling is "always paint everything, even if the plastic is the right color." Bare plastic has an unnatural soapy sheen that is never realistic.

Most armor models come molded in colors that are at least close to the colors used on the real vehicle, but that doesn't mean you don't have to paint them. In fact, the surest giveaway that a finished model was built by a novice is raw, unpainted plastic. Even if the plastic does happen to be the right color, bare plastic has an unmistakable — and unrealistic — waxy sheen. For this reason, the first rule to follow in painting your armor models is this: ALWAYS PAINT EVERYTHING.

As models go, armor models are about the easiest to paint. They are frequently one color overall, and when camouflage patterns are required, they are rarely difficult, even for a beginner. And, there are no advanced painting techniques for armor, only more practiced applications of the basic techniques that we'll talk about in this chapter.

The most important choice you have to make in painting is whether to spray or use a brush. Although brushing will get the job done, because of the numerous nooks and crannies in armor models spraying is easier and more effective. A tank that takes an hour to paint with a brush can be sprayed in about 5 minutes — with better coverage, to boot. I'm sold on spray painting for armor models, even for beginners, so I'll devote most of the discussion here to spray painting techniques.

Types of paint. There are many types and brands of hobby paints to choose from. Enamels — among them, Testor, Pactra, and Humbrol — thin with turpentine or mineral spirits and have been considered standard paints for plastic modeling for years. They work well, but require a day or two to dry hard before you can do any heavy weathering over them.

Lacquer-type paints such as Floquil and other model railroad colors spray beautifully, and because of their solvent action they really bite into the surface of the plastic and take hold. That same solvent action, however, makes lacquers generally unsuitable for brushing or aerosol use — with those application methods the paint remains wet for too long, giving the solvent time to eat away, or "craze," the surface of the model. Barrier coats are available to minimize this problem, but lacquer paints are best applied with an airbrush.

Water-base model paints, such as Polly S, brush on beautifully, cover in one coat, and can be weathered immediately without danger of lifting. These paints have been steadily gaining in popularity over the past several years.

Choosing the right colors. Over the years, more hot air has been generated about correct colors than any other phase of armor modeling. As a newcomer, it's easy to be confused by all the controversy, so I'll try to provide an overall perspective here.

What all the hot air eventually boils down to is this: There are no absolutely correct colors for a particular vehicle. Aside from concocting your own colors out of thin air, perhaps the biggest error you can make is to adhere fanatically to colors from photos, drawings, or even color chips. When choosing colors you should examine all the color references you can find, form a personal impression from all that you have seen, and work from that. You'll rarely be very far off, and most of the time you'll be right on the money.

Why not accept color references at face value? First, color reproduction in any book, including this one, is never 100 percent accurate. Second, weathering causes colors to fade and change, so no two vehicles in the field will ever be exactly the same color, even if they were painted the same color at the same time. Finally, the human eye reacts differently to colors on large and small objects at varying distances, so

in the real world the exact same color can actually look different.

Even colors issued or specified by the government are rarely uniform. I recall an occasion in Germany when the order came down to paint out the white stars on our U. S. vehicles. We had an alert the next day, and as I watched the tanks and armored personnel carriers rolling out the gate it struck me that no two shades of olive drab paint used for the job were the same; the colors ranged from khaki to near-black, and not one of them was a match for the overall color of the vehicle.

German WWII armor colors are also far from an exact science. The dark gray used early in the war was highly susceptible to weathering, and thus varied considerably from one vehicle to the next. Late in the war the Germans switched to a basic factory-applied dark tan, and issued their reddish-brown and olive green camouflage colors in concentrated paste form for application in the field. The paste was to be thinned with either water or gasoline, and the amount of thinner used greatly affected the resulting colors — thick paints yielded chocolate brown and dark green, while much-thinned applications resulted in brick red and pea green. To further complicate the situation, troops in the field also used captured supplies or whatever else came their way.

So, within certain commonsense limitations, you have a good deal of leeway when it comes to choosing "the right color" for a particular vehicle. The color samples on page 12 show several basic colors and provide a good place to start, but in view of what I've

Paints suitable for armor modeling include Floquil (lacquer), Testor and Pactra (enamel), and Polly S (water-base). All are available at most hobby shops.

The type of airbrush sold at hobby shops is all you need for modeling (below). Instead of buying empty paint bottles to use as paint containers, I mounted the siphon top for the airbrush in a snap-on cap from a disposable rubber film canister (above).

COLORS FOR ARMORED VEHICLES

These are hardly the last words in vehicle colors, but they are representative, and good basic color references.

GERMAN
Panzer
Sand
(1943-45)

GERMAN
Red-brown
camouflage
(1943-45)

GERMAN
Green
camouflage
(1943-45)
also
BRITISH and
RUSSIAN
Green

GERMAN
Panzer
Gray
(1939-43)

U.S. WWII
Olive drab
(1940-50)

U.S. WWII
Olive-
green

U.S., other
countries
modern
olive drab

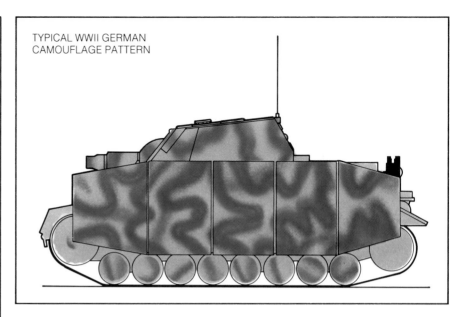

TYPICAL WWII GERMAN
CAMOUFLAGE PATTERN

said above, you need not feel constrained to follow them too religiously!

Preparing the model for painting. Before painting, remove the tracks and break the model down into subassemblies. Then clean them.

Plastic kit manufacturers spray their molds with silicone parting agents to keep the plastic parts from sticking, and residue from these parting agents can keep paint from sticking to your model. Simply washing the model will eliminate the silicone residue and remove finger oils and plastic shavings deposited during assembly. Immerse each subassembly in warm water and dishwashing detergent, scrub lightly with a soft brush, rinse thoroughly, and set the pieces aside to dry.

About airbrushes and air supplies. The best way to paint an armor model is with an airbrush. An airbrush is nothing more than a miniature paint sprayer, and its chief advantages are that you can spray any color you want, and that you have precise control of the spray pressure and amount of paint being applied. With an airbrush you'll be able to apply thin, even overall color coats, and to spray intricate camouflage patterns. An airbrush system consists of an air supply, an air hose, the airbrush itself, and a siphon bottle for paint.

If you're at all serious about modeling you'll own an airbrush sooner or later; if you can afford it, it might as well be sooner. You don't need an expensive airbrush or air supply for most modelwork, and entirely adequate systems are less expensive than you might think. A standard Binks, Badger, or Paasche hobby airbrush is all you need — leave the expensive turbine models for the photo retouch specialists!

There are several choices for an air supply. Most hobby shops sell aerosol cans of airbrush propellant, and these are a good way to get started. Each can holds enough propellant to last an average hobbyist a month or two. When you find yourself using several cans of propellant in a comparatively short period, it's time to think about investing in a compressor or a carbon dioxide tank.

The CO_2 tank brings with it the advantage of allowing precise regulation of the air pressure, an important consideration for fine detail work, but you must have the tank refilled periodically. The compressor is noisy, but it is always ready when you need it. Yet another source of compressed gas is an automobile inner tube (hobby shops sell adapter fittings to hook the tube to your airbrush). The disadvantage of the inner tube is that its capacity is severely limited; the pressure drops off rapidly and you have to keep reinflating it.

If you find yourself doing a lot of spraying, you should consider adding a spray booth, either homemade or commercial, to your workshop. I don't have one; in fact, I usually spray paint my models over a wastebasket! Whether you opt for a spray booth or not, if you are at all susceptible to toxic fumes or are allergic to dust, a simple face mask is a must.

Painting with an airbrush. Airbrush painting requires that the paint be thinned. Although the manufacturers' recommended paint dilutions for airbrushing vary from brand to brand, a good rule of thumb is to cut the paint about 30 percent with thinner from its normal brushing consistency. For airbrushing, thin Polly S with rubbing alcohol instead of water.

Spray a few test patterns on pieces of scrap cardboard, adjusting the paint control and air pressure for optimum coverage. Start with the paint control open all the way, and gradually tighten it down until the paint dries almost as soon as it touches the surface being sprayed.

For overall coverage, work with the paint control at a medium setting, holding the airbrush 6″ to 9″ from the surface. Vary the paint control setting and the distance between the brush and the work until you obtain good coverage with two or three passes and without puddling the paint. Lacquers should dry to the touch almost on contact, and enamels and water-base paints shouldn't take much longer.

Airbrushes work best if they are kept clean, but you don't have to be a fanatic about it. When I change colors or finish an airbrushing session I slip a bottle of thinner onto the brush and spray until the result is clear. After every other session or so, or when the airbrush won't be used for a while, I take it apart for a thorough cleaning.

Painting with spray cans. If you are not ready to invest in an airbrush, aerosol spray cans will also do the job, though not as well. Spray cans are convenient, but the disadvantages are that your choice of colors is limited and you have no control over the amount of paint or pressure.

There are a few tricks to obtaining good results with spray cans. Always shake the can thoroughly before painting, and test each can on scrap cardboard to ensure that the paint is completely mixed and to determine the best working distance. If you hold the spray can too close to the model the paint will puddle and drip; too far away, and it won't cover. When spraying aim off to one side of the vehicle, press the button, then move the spray across the surface, depositing a thin, even coat.

Several spray passes from different angles are usually necessary for each side of a vehicle, and several light coats are better than one heavy one. Be careful not to allow too much buildup of wet paint; if the paint looks as if it is going to puddle or drip, stop and let the model dry before continuing. If drips do occur, wipe them off quickly with a tissue, then spray over the area again before it has a chance to dry. You can obtain a finer spray if you immerse the can for a few minutes in warm (not hot) water to heat the contents slightly.

Brush painting. Even if you use an airbrush or spray cans for most painting, certain small details still have to be touched in with a brush. The best brushes for detailing are round red sable artist's brushes. Choose a brush that holds a decent amount of paint; I avoid the super-tiny No. 000 and No. 0000 sizes in favor of a No. 0 or No. 1 with a well-pointed tip. It is the shape of the brush tip that is important, not the size.

If you decide to paint overall vehicle colors with a brush, the best choice is a wide, flat, red sable artist's brush. Such brushes are expensive, so take care of them and clean them thoroughly after each use.

Polly S yields the best finish if you must paint with a brush, although enamels also work well if you are careful. The key to all good brush painting, whether overall painting of an entire vehicle or delicate detail painting, is controlling the consistency of the paint. If the paint is too thin it will not cover properly and will run where you don't want it; if it is too thick, it will gum up the brush, leave heavy brush marks, and not cover well either. When the

When painting with a spray can, start the spray off to one side of the model and then move it quickly across the surface. Stop well beyond the model.

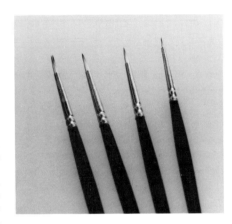

Quality brushes are important for brush painting. Use red sable flats for broad areas, and rounds like these for detail.

The trick to brush painting is to never paint directly out of the bottle. Transfer the paint to a palette where you can control its consistency, then paint from that.

consistency is just right, paint will flow from the brush like ink from a fountain pen, covering smoothly in one coat.

Controlling paint consistency is a matter of following just one simple rule: Never paint directly from the bottle. Always transfer paint to a separate container or a piece of glass and test its brushing qualities on scrap material. If the paint is too thin, let it sit a few minutes to thicken by evaporation; if it is too thick, add a little thinner. As you work, occasionally add a

PRESSURE TOO LOW, paint does not atomize properly, spatters.

PAINT TOO THIN, sprays well, but will not cover, may run before drying.

PAINT TOO THICK, airbrush clogs easily, paint dries too quickly, comes out in irregular bursts.

COMMON AIRBRUSH PROBLEMS

TOO THICK, paint clogs brush, covers surface in blobs, leaves brush marks.

JUST RIGHT, paint flows freely from brush to model, covers well, brush marks blend in and disappear.

TOO THIN, paint doesn't cover raised detail.

EXAMPLES OF PAINT CONSISTENCY

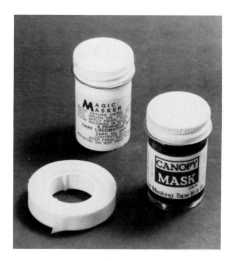

Masking tape is good for straight line applications, but a liquid rubber mask is superior for intricate curves or highly detailed surfaces.

drop of thinner to maintain the proper paint consistency.

Brush using broad strokes, spreading the paint gently and evenly across the surface. Cross-hatching — brushing first in one direction, then perpendicular to it — is helpful in minimizing brush marks. Try not to miss spots, because areas touched up after the main coat of paint has dried will always show. Some colors, particularly light colors over dark, simply won't cover in one coat no matter what you do. In such cases, two or even three thin coats are better than a single heavy one.

Masking. Masking is seldom called for on armor models, but when it is, there are only a few rules to follow.

First, never apply masking tape until the paint surface has had at least 24 hours to set. Otherwise, the tape may lift the paint.

If your tape must be cut in patterns, never cut the tape on the model, since doing so would scribe the surface of the plastic, leaving marks that would be accentuated by weathering. Instead, cut the tape to approximate size and shape on a cutting board, using several overlapping tape strips if necessary. Test the fit, mark adjustments on the tape with a pencil, return to the cutting board, and trim.

When applying masking tape, rub the edges down tightly to keep paint from creeping underneath. When brush painting, carefully peel off the tape while the paint is still wet; this helps prevent a hard ridge of paint from forming along the masked edge.

Quick, simple masks for spray painting can be cut from paper (tissue, towel, or writing paper, depending on the desired edge). Wet the paper and allow the moisture to hold it in place on the model while you spray.

Liquid rubber masking compounds are particularly useful where heavily contoured or detailed surfaces must be masked. Your hobby shop should have the commercial rubber masking solutions offered for modeling, or you can use ordinary rubber cement. After applying the liquid to the model with a brush, cut the rubber (being careful not to cut the plastic underneath) with a knife and peel off the unwanted portion. When the paint is dry the mask can be delicately peeled off with a knife or rubbed off with a pencil eraser. Liquid masks are particularly effective for modeling chipped paint and other weathering applications. We'll come back to them in Chapter 3.

Armor camouflage patterns. Camouflage on armored vehicles ranges from the fairly random patterns applied to WWII German armor in the field to the regulation patterns and colors specified for today's U. S. vehicles. Camouflage paint is applied to real tanks in several different ways — factories, repair depots, and field maintenance units generally have spray equipment, but vehicle crews usually have to settle for brushes, or even mops. (As usual, there's an exception. In WWII, German units were issued spray guns that operated off the vehicle's air compressor!)

Wartime camouflage schemes rarely corresponded to those specified in regulations, and the regulations intentionally gave field units broad leeway to apply camouflage as local conditions required. Peacetime camouflage is likely to be far more uniform, but not entirely so. For instance, although camouflage patterns are specified for each type of U. S. Army vehicle, I have discovered that troops are encouraged to

vary the pattern from one vehicle to the next, using the published schemes only as a guide.

The easiest way to model sprayed camouflage patterns is with an airbrush. Adjust the airbrush down to a fine pattern (you may have to thin the paint more than usual, and increase the pressure slightly), and spray on the pattern you like. If you make a mistake, go back and touch it up with the original color.

Another technique for simulating sprayed camouflage is to punch or cut irregular holes in a piece of cardboard. Hold the card near (but not touching) the surface of the model and spray, either with an airbrush or spray can. Yet another method, somewhat cruder, is to glue little balls of cotton to the surface of the vehicle with white glue. Spray the surface, and then remove the cotton balls with water.

Although smooth, regular patterns can be masked and sprayed, the best way to model hard-edged camouflage applied with a brush or mop is brushing. For a "mopped-on" look, use a ratty old paintbrush to literally smear the paint around, just as was done on the actual vehicle.

Painting road wheels and tracks. When the camouflage is finished, it's time to paint the running gear. Most, but not all, tracked vehicles have black rubber tires on the road wheels and return rollers.

If you glued the wheels in place, painting the tires can be an exercise in frustration, but if you left them free-turning, the job is almost a snap. Set the vehicle on its side, touch a brush full of paint to the tire with the tip of the brush just touching the inner edge, and touch one finger of the same hand to the model to steady the brush in just the right position. Now use your other hand to slowly turn the wheel, keeping the brush stationary. For practice, paint the inside of each wheel first. After just one or two tries you can turn out a perfectly painted wheel every time.

The tracks are the only parts of full-size tracked vehicles that are left unpainted and allowed to rust. Tracks are subject to such extremes of dirt, rust, and grime that painting them actually comes under the heading of weathering (Chapter 3), but you will need some sort of basic color to work on, so paint them an overall dark rust brown. Do not paint them gunmetal gray or iron (or, horror of horrors, silver!) unless you are out to model a vehicle literally rolling off the assembly line.

Since 1945, most tracked vehicles have incorporated black rubber tread "shoes," which permit longer track life and cause less damage to roads during peacetime. Sometimes, the only visible metal parts are guide teeth and track connectors. When modeling a vehicle

Some WWII German armor crews could paint their tanks by hooking up a spray gun to the vehicle's air compressor.

One method for spraying camouflage is to spray through holes punched in an index card. Since holes have to be punched near the edge, tape another card to the edge to prevent overspray.

Road wheels that are left free to turn are easy to paint. Rotate the wheel with one hand while holding the brush steady with the other. Not all tanks have rubber tires, but most do.

that has rubber-shoe tracks, paint the tracks black overall, then go back and paint the metal parts dark brown with a brush.

Painting interiors. If your vehicle will have open hatches, some of the interior will be visible. In general, any part of an armored vehicle visible from the ground or air, including the insides of hatches and open crew compartments, is painted the vehicle camouflage color. The actual enclosed interior, however, is usually painted a light color for maximum illumination and visibility when the vehicle is buttoned up. The most common interior color is white, but many WWII German interiors were light cream accentuated with reddish-brown primer and dark gray, while American interiors have been pale lime green since the early '60s.

The easiest way to paint interiors is spraying, usually before the rest of the vehicle is painted. Because access to the interior becomes restricted as you build the model, you may have to paint some surfaces before or even during assembly. Keep this in mind as you preplan the assembly sequence for any model with open hatches.

Detail painting. Nearly everything on armored vehicles is painted the basic camouflage color (including stowed tools, which are often left in place when the vehicle rolls into the spray booth) so there is relatively little detail painting on an armor model. The items that require separate painting include machine guns, lights, instruments, and fire extinguishers.

Machine guns, including the bow gun on tanks, are usually blued steel, while their mounts and cradles are painted. To bring out the detail on machine guns paint them black, then lightly dry-brush with gunmetal (to find instructions on dry-brushing, skip ahead to Chapter 3).

Don't paint headlights white; instead, use silver, or better yet, gun-metal with a silver highlight across the top of the lens. Similarly, don't paint taillights bright red; use dark red (look at the ones on your car).

You can mask off details and spray them, but given a little practice and a good brush you should be able to do the job faster by hand. The key to detail painting is the same golden rule for brush painting that I mentioned earlier: NEVER PAINT DIRECTLY OUT OF THE BOTTLE. For good detail work, you must have complete control of the consistency of the paint, so it's crucial that you always transfer a small quantity of paint to a separate container or a piece of cardboard or glass, and work from that.

Once you have the paint thinned or thickened to the proper consistency, painting fine detail is a lot like firing a rifle: Exhale, hold your breath, relax, and paint.

Working with decals. Decals in armor kits are not as numerous nor as colorful as those on aircraft, but how you apply them is actually more critical, because subsequent weathering will bring out every flaw.

Decals adhere best to glossy surfaces, but therein lies a problem: Most model paints yield a flat finish, almost like very fine sandpaper, which decals have a hard time snuggling down against. If you apply decals directly over flat paint the result will be tiny white air bubbles under the clear decal film when it dries. Glossy surfaces are microscopically smooth, so air bubbles are not so likely to form between them and the decal film.

One solution to this problem is to apply a patch of clear gloss varnish wherever a decal is to be applied. Another approach, one I use often, is to paint the entire vehicle with gloss paint, then give it a final coat of matte varnish after the decals have been applied.

Before applying any decal, trim as much of the excess clear film from the edges of the decal as you can. That excess film may not be visible on a freshly finished model, but weathering often makes decal film reappear as if by magic — unwanted magic!

Always use a setting solution such as MicroSet or Solvaset. These solutions soften the decal film, allowing the decal, as it dries, to stretch and shrink onto the surface of the model. This is particularly important when decals must be positioned over hinges

Always trim the excess clear decal film from around the design when using decals other than those from Microscale.

After soaking an individual decal from its backing paper, handle and position it with a brush. Add a drop or two of water to the area if the decal doesn't slide freely, then blot the water away when you have it where you want it. Using a decal-setting solution will ensure that the film snuggles down tightly around raised details.

Dry transfers are hard to work with because you can't adjust their position. However, they have no telltale film, and look terrific once in place. You can enjoy some of the best of both worlds by rubbing them onto decal paper, then applying them as you would regular decals.

Even if you want to model sloppy hand lettering, for best results use decals and then go back and add a few drips and intentional errors with a pointed brush.

Matte varnish can be temperamental, so find a brand that you like and stick with it. Even then, always test it on something else before spraying it on a completed model as a final flat coating.

or other raised detail. If you find white spots under the decals after the setting solution has dried, prick each spot several times with the point of your modeling knife and brush on more setting solution.

One decal manufacturer, Super Scale International (formerly Microscale), offers a "disappearing film" decal system that works very well for armor.* The key to the system is that Microscale decal film is soluble in MicroCoat varnish. The decal is applied over a coat of MicroCoat Gloss, then oversprayed with another coat, which dissolves the edge of the film into the bottom layer, leaving an invisible border. A coat of MicroCoat Flat finishes the job. I use Microscale decals whenever possible.

Dry transfers and hand lettering.

* Super Scale International, 2211 Mouton, Carson City, NV 89706.

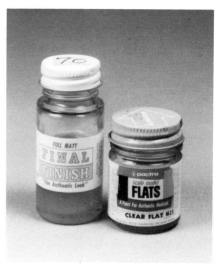

Dry transfers, also called rub-on decals, offer an alternative to decals. These have no clear film to worry about, but are difficult to apply to contoured or textured surfaces and cannot be repositioned if they are applied crooked. A simple solution to the problem of repositioning is to rub the dry transfer onto a sheet of plain decal paper, such as the clear border from a standard decal sheet, then soak it off and apply it as a regular decal. One-piece designs, such as white stars or German vehicle numbers, can usually be transferred to bare (no film) decal paper, but words and signs should be transferred to paper with film on it so the design will hold together. (Otherwise, the parts of the design would drift apart as soon as they float free of the paper.)

Finally, a word of warning about hand-painted vehicle numbers and insignia. Such painting was common practice among front-line troops of all armies, and some of the results were pretty crude. In theory, crude hand lettering might seem like a nice personal touch for a model, but in practice it turns out to be more difficult than it sounds. The trick is to make the imperfections appear intentional on your part, not accidental, and this requires an artist's eye and some carefully orchestrated and controlled drips and errors to carry it off well.

Unfortunately, the usual result of hand-painted lettering is that people viewing your model will conclude you tried to get away without buying decals and botched the job. If you must model hand lettering, the best method is to apply decals as usual, then go back and carefully paint in a few drips and irregularities after the decals dry. The result is neater and more regular than you could do by hand, but still clearly hand-lettered by the crew.

The final touch. After all painting, decaling, and detail painting are complete, the final touch is to spray your model with a coat of clear flat varnish. The matte coating "kills" glossy or semigloss surfaces, providing a realistic overall dead-flat finish on your model as well as a slightly frosted texture that will be useful when applying weathering.

Flat finishes can be very temperamental to work with. They should be sprayed on, not brushed, and in my experience they can suddenly go "bad" (turn glossy or semigloss) on the shelf. Before using a flat finish make sure it is thoroughly mixed, and always test it on scrap before applying it to a model. If the test doesn't dry dead flat, don't use it. Mix the varnish thoroughly, try again, and if it still doesn't dry dead flat, throw it out and buy some more. After spraying the model give the varnish at least two days to harden fully before you begin weathering.

This model, Steve Zaloga's amazing scratchbuilt 1/76 scale M1 Abrams Main Battle Tank, has been airbrushed with a basic overall coat of Forest Green, then painted with one of the modern U. S. MERDC (Mobility Equipment Research and Development Command) four-color schemes. Now it's ready for weathering. Photo by Steve Zaloga.

As well as contributing to realism, weathering helps show off the detail on armor models.

3
Weathering

Tanks attract dirt like small children, and this U. S. Army Signal Corps photo of a tank destroyer in late 1944 shows the result. Note the mud encrusting the entire lower portion of the vehicle, the water stains on the sides and the bedrolls, and the oil that has leaked from spare cans carried on various parts of the vehicle. An interesting feature is the tarp spread over the top of the open turret to keep out the rain.

Tanks love dirt. They wallow in it. They don't move over the terrain so much as they move through it, joyfully spreading mud, dust, and dirt all over themselves and the surrounding countryside. Weathering is an essential aspect of armor modeling, and if you build only clean tank models you not only fail to do justice to the true nature of these wondrous beasts, but you're missing half the fun!

The causes of weathering. In this chapter we'll restrict ourselves to the everyday varieties of wear and tear that occur as much in peacetime as in war. Later on, in Chapter 10, we'll deal with the heaviest weathering effects of all, battle damage.

The first consideration in weathering a particular model is the sort of service the vehicle has supposedly seen. For example, Panther tanks from the battle of Kursk, where the Panther was first introduced, would not be nearly as worn and battered as those used in the Normandy campaign. A tank that has spent its career in the rocky, dusty terrain of the Western Desert will look much different from one that has served its time wallowing in the swamp mud around Leningrad.

(Left) Tanks are designed to move through the terrain as well as over it. Although it doesn't take much mud to make a mess of the running gear, a lot of mud can really do the job (right). It's hard to believe these German transports could move at all!

Some vehicles had such short combat careers that they never had much of a chance to get dirty at all. Many of the T-34s that the Russians threw into their desperate frontal attacks in 1942 went into battle directly off flatcars from the factory, and some were even knocked out before they could use a full tank of gas.

The best way to learn about weathering is to study photos of real vehicles on campaign in different parts of the world. If there is an army post near your home, it's well worth your while to go out and study the real thing.

Paint fading, failure, and rust. Most of the surface of any military vehicle is painted to protect against rust and to hinder enemy observation. This paint never stays entirely intact for long, because it is subject to a variety of destructive forces.

The first is the sun, which, particularly in the desert, fades the paint on all surfaces exposed to its rays, and weakens the paint, making it more likely to flake and peel.

Second are the crewmen, who must climb all over the vehicle not only to maintain it, but just to get inside. There are convenient and inconvenient ways to climb aboard; the most favored routes will be marked by worn paint. Similar scuffing will be found around crew hatches, engine compartments, and fuel filler caps.

Paint scuffs off edges and projections before damage shows on flat surfaces. Areas that suffer constant wear will show bright metal where the paint has worn through, but those subject to only occasional abuse will rust over, and rainwater will eventually wash small streaks of rust down the side of the vehicle. Rust isn't always appropriate, though; some modern vehicles, including the U. S. M113, use aluminum alloy armor, and aluminum doesn't rust!

Heat and moisture. Most vulnerable to rust are the exhaust system and the tracks. Because external exhaust systems are subject to a combination of heat and moisture they deteriorate quickly. First paint blisters off, then the surface rusts, and since mufflers are not usually armored, the thin sheet metal eventually rusts through, leaving pits and ragged holes in the surface.

The parts of the vehicle subject to intense heat and flame, the exhausts and gun muzzle, are usually blackened with scorched paint and soot. Sometimes a little detective work is required to find the exhausts on your model — they aren't always pipes, and they emerge in different locations on different vehicles. On Shermans the exhausts were tucked under the back of the rear deck; on modern vehicles they are located behind grilles or louvers on the back, top, or sides.

The track is usually the only part of a vehicle that is not painted at all. Even in peacetime, track parts quickly acquire an overall coating of dark rust, which wears off only those areas that come in contact with the ground or the running gear. These will re-rust bright orange overnight, only to be worn smooth again the next day. So, track shows three separate weathering effects — old rust, fresh rust, and bare metal.

Mud, dust, grease, and oil. A tank traveling down a muddy road churns up mud like a Waring blender. One layer of mud dries on top of another, encrusting the entire undercarriage and suspension system with successive layers that can build up to a foot thick. Even the lightest tracked vehicle crossing a grassy field will destroy all turf in its path, leaving parallel swaths of churned-up brown earth in its wake. The torn-up sod is quickly plastered throughout the vehicle's suspension system, adding bits of grass and leaves to the accumulated mud.

Any tanker can tell you how much hard work is involved after returning to garrison from the field to chisel and hose off two weeks' accumulation of dried mud.

Dust is often associated only with the desert, but dust is a nuisance anywhere it hasn't rained in the past week. During the summer, that includes a good part of the known world. Tanks throw up dust clouds which settle all over the vehicle and crew. Wind, crew activity, and even brushing by tree branches remove most of it, but it remains in corners, nooks, and crannies where it is less likely to be brushed or blown off.

Grease and oil stains aren't particularly prominent on armor because such stains are quickly covered by dust. The occasional bad bearing seal on a road wheel or torsion bar shows up as an irregular dark stain in the surrounding dust.

Winter camouflage. Snow camouflage is applied so haphazardly and is subject to such extreme weathering that I consider it under the category of weathering. While special white camouflage paint is sometimes issued, as often as not ordinary whitewash is pressed into service, usually applied with brushes, rags, mops, or in sheer desperation, simply poured over the vehicle. Since even issue winter colors are not intended to be permanent, the white does not last long, quickly deteriorating to a dingy gray accented with splashes of mud and patches where the original color wears through.

Armor weathering techniques. Every modeler has his own favorite weathering techniques, and as you gain experience, you'll develop your own. I will discuss four techniques in detail, and on most vehicles you will probably use them all, in roughly the order I describe them.

It's important to realize that weathering techniques aren't cut-and-dried. There will be times when you skip a step, do things in a different order, or use techniques to achieve effects different from those discussed here. Don't worry about it. There are no hard and fast rules in weathering — the results are what count, and whatever methods work for you are the "right" ones.

Step 1: Washes. The first step in weathering is to apply a wash over the basic paint. This wash is nothing more than greatly thinned paint flowed over the surface so color accumulates in corners and recesses. Although the primary purpose of this technique is to accent surface relief and bring out detail, washes can also be used to simulate oil, grease, and other stains, and to alter base colors.

Certain paints and thinners are best for washes. Lacquers don't make good washes, because they may soften or lift the paint they are applied over. Washes made from water-base paints have a peculiar habit of looking great when you first apply them, but they often dry blotchy and unattractive. My top choices for washes are paints thinned with turpentine or mineral spirits: flat hobby enamels such as Humbrol, Pactra, or Testor, and artist's oil paints. You should experiment with various paints and thinners until you find the ones you like best.

To apply a wash, first give your model a light overall brushing with thinner to prepare the surface. While this dries, make the wash itself by mixing a small amount of color with a lot of thinner. Exact proportions aren't important — what you really want is not thinned paint, but tinted thinner. To accentuate detail, make the wash with a darker shade of the basic model color (you can use black, but it's better to add some of the basic model color to black).

Use a wide, soft brush to flow the wash freely onto the model, letting it run into all the small cracks and crevices. Apply the wash to large, clearly defined sections of the model such as the rear deck, side, or turret; working on small, undefined areas results in blotchy patches with irregular borders of paint around them when dry. Excess wash can be soaked up with a paper towel, but be sure to leave a generous accumulation in the recesses. While the wash is still wet you may want to wipe some areas clean with a dry tissue or cloth.

Use darker concentrated washes to simulate oil and grease stains. Apply these with a brush, streaking the stains downward if they would run and leaving irregular blotches if they would not. Try applying two or three different colored stains to adjoining areas at the same time, allowing them to flow together at the edges for an interesting effect.

Alternate wash techniques. Occasionally, washes give both beginning and experienced modelers a hard time, most often by drying as a blotchy mess. If you encounter this problem,

there are a couple of ways around it. One alternate wash technique is to mix finely ground pastel chalk powder (see page 22) with thinner, brushing it on just as you would a paint wash. When the thinner dries the chalk powder won't blow away, but it is loose enough that the surface can be wiped fairly clean if you don't like the result.

Another approach is to use the antiquing stains sold in plaster craft shops. These stains come in several colors and have a longer working time than a paint stain as well as a thicker, stickier consistency than paint.

The trick in using antiquing stain as a wash is to apply the stain, then wipe most of it off. I prefer to use cloth instead of tissue for this wiping, since it will not tear on raised detail or leave lint on the model. I use two pieces of cloth, one dry, the other dampened with mineral spirits for use when the antiquing stain starts to dry and thicken. Cotton swabs help in tight places. By rubbing lightly with a circular motion, you can break up the evenness of the color even on broad flat surfaces, creating subtle darkening effects. The only disadvantage of antiquing stains is that they dry glossy, requiring an overspray of flat varnish.

Whatever you use for washes, be careful not to overdo them; you want a darker color in the recesses — but not straight black. Later, when you dry-brush the model, the contrast between raised and recessed detail will be increased, and what may look like insufficient contrast after the wash alone may later turn out to be just right. When weathering, it's always better to err on the side of subtlety.

Step 2: Dry-brushing. This is the technique of lightly whisking an almost-dry brush back and forth across the surface of the model to apply a "frosting" of paint to raised detail.

The best brush for dry-brushing is a flat red sable, about ½" wide. The two factors that control the effect are the amount of paint on the brush and the consistency of the paint. If there is too much paint on the brush it will leave solid patches of color instead of a light frosting; if there is too little paint, the brush will leave nothing at all. I regulate the amount of paint by stroking the brush back and forth on a scrap of cardboard or cloth before touching it to the model.

Paint consistency is important because even when you have the right amount of paint on the brush, if the paint is too thin dry-brushing will leave unrealistic streaks. Paint that is too thick will be reluctant to leave the brush and will be deposited in rough, chunky blobs. Control paint consistency as described in Chapter 2: Remove a small quantity from the bottle and thin or thicken it as required.

The desired result of dry-brushing is

When applying a wash, work one section of the model at a time and let the thinned paint accumulate in the recesses, directing it there with a brush (above). Excess wash can be wiped off with tissue (below).

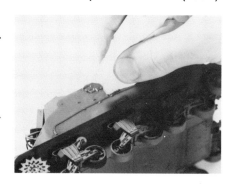

a smooth, subtle gradation of color, and the type of paint you use has a lot to do with the result. I like artist's oil paints, but they take much longer to dry than hobby paints. Many modelers achieve superb results with straight hobby enamels, still others mix oils half and half with them. Water-base paints can also be used; here again, I suggest you experiment with several

Dry-brushing is particularly effective for bringing out subtle detail such as that on the floor of the fighting compartment of the Italeri Priest (above) and emphasizing the tools stowed on the rear deck (below).

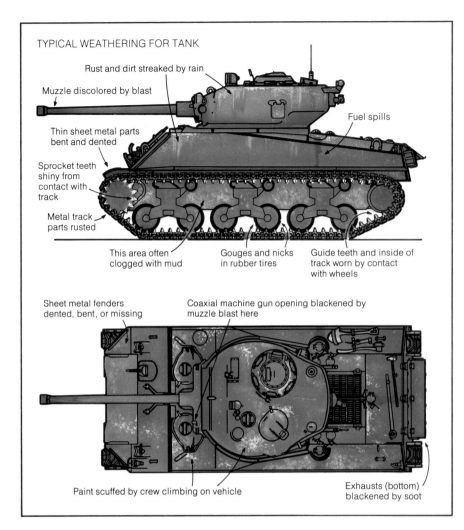

TYPICAL WEATHERING FOR TANK

Rust and dirt streaked by rain

Muzzle discolored by blast

Fuel spills

Thin sheet metal parts bent and dented

Sprocket teeth shiny from contact with track

Metal track parts rusted

This area often clogged with mud

Gouges and nicks in rubber tires

Guide teeth and inside of track worn by contact with wheels

Sheet metal fenders dented, bent, or missing

Coaxial machine gun opening blackened by muzzle blast here

Paint scuffed by crew climbing on vehicle

Exhausts (bottom) blackened by soot

The winter camouflage being applied to this Sherman is whitewash, done in a semi-covering pattern suited to wooded terrain. Units in the field used brushes, mops, and even rags for painting.

paints before settling on a personal favorite.

Colors for dry-brushing vary from one model to the next. If your model has a camouflage pattern, you will have to dry-brush the base color and each of the camouflage colors separately. A good color to start with is a lighter shade of the basic color on the model. Add white to the basic color, adjust the consistency of the paint, and pick up just a little paint on the brush.

Then work most of the paint off the brush on cardboard or a rag, and begin stroking it back and forth over the surface of the model. In some areas you'll have to use a scrubbing action to get the right effect.

After dry-brushing the entire model once, add more white to the paint and repeat the process, this time stroking more lightly and catching only the raised detail. Step back, examine your work critically, and dry-brush again

with an even lighter color if necessary. Engraved detail which was barely visible before dry-brushing should now be highlighted beautifully.

Dry-brushed dirt, rust, and bare metal. The next step is to repeat the dry-brushing treatment with an earth color (either mud or dust), gradually lightening it as you did the basic model color. Lightly apply the earth color in irregular blotches, bearing in mind that dirt is most prevalent on the parts of the vehicle near the ground. To avoid a monochromatic look and give the model a realistic "spark," vary the color, adding small amounts of brown to the color here, touches of green there. A nice touch when simulating wet mud is to counterpoint it with a bit of much lighter dried mud higher up on the vehicle.

A good example of grease stains done with washes on Jim Stephens' scratchbuilt Mark IV. Also note the subtle rust streaks.

The muffler on this Monogram Stug IV was dented with a motor tool and knife, coated with liquid cement and dipped in baking soda to add texture, and finally painted and dry-brushed with various rusty shades of red, orange, and dark brown.

Wet mud is evenly spread all over the underside of this 1/25 scale Mack truck by Jim Stephens, but note how the rain has washed and streaked it along the side of the tank.

Francois Verlinden has brought out the grille of this vehicle by dry-brushing, and added dust, paint discoloration, and faint rust streaks around the headlights, bolts, and screws with washes.

Effective dry-brushing, more than any other weathering technique, is a matter of "fiddlin' around" until the model looks right. You may dry-brush the same area half a dozen times before you achieve just the effect that pleases you, so don't be afraid to experiment — it's the only way to learn any weathering technique.

To weather the tracks, start by dry-brushing the metal parts with progressively lighter shades of rust brown. Then dry-brush only the highlights with gunmetal. Pay particular attention to the inside surface of each track; the sides of the guide teeth should be worn bright, as should the flat portion of all-metal track that comes in contact with the road wheels.

Also dry-brush gunmetal on the rims of metal road wheels and idlers, and the teeth on drive sprockets. A good substitute for gunmetal paint is powdered graphite; rubbing parts with a very soft (No. 0) lead pencil also works. Finish the tracks by dry-brushing the whole assembly, both metal and rubber portions, with several shades of dust or mud.

The final step in dry-brushing is to add scuff marks where paint has worn down to bare metal. Again use gunmetal paint, but with more of a stabbing, stippling motion of the brush. Keep in mind that paint scuffs off in small scratches, not whole sections, and that such damage is usually limited to a few well-traveled areas of the vehicle. The biggest mistake beginners make is overdoing it; when you reach the point where it looks as if a few more strokes of the brush will do it, stop — it's just right the way it is.

When you are satisfied with your dry-brushed effects, allow several days for the paint to set. Once the dry-brushed color is completely cured you can apply washes over it to tone it

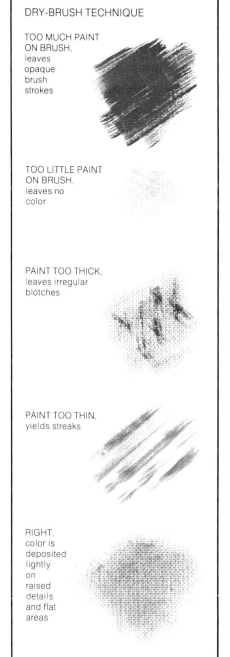

DRY-BRUSH TECHNIQUE

TOO MUCH PAINT ON BRUSH, leaves opaque brush strokes

TOO LITTLE PAINT ON BRUSH, leaves no color

PAINT TOO THICK, leaves irregular blotches

PAINT TOO THIN, yields streaks

RIGHT, color is deposited lightly on raised details and flat areas

Dry-brushing needn't always be done with light colors. Here, Bob Dye has used a dark brown, almost-black color to give a realistic ground-in dirt look to his Italeri Hetzer.

Two examples of really effective dry-brushing by Dave Smith. In the photo above, note the way the dry-brushing brings out the detail on the tracks, running gear, and raised details on the hull of this Panzer IV, including the rusty texture of the muffler. The subject of the photo below, a Russian KV-1 by Tamiya, is deceptively simple-looking and seemingly devoid of much surface texture or detail. Here the dry-brushing has emphasized the blocky shape of the vehicle by highlighting the contours and edges, particularly around the turret, and also shows off the detail that is present to best advantage.

down. Add washes only if you feel the dry-brushing is too harsh or the color isn't quite right.

Step 3: Hazing, feathering, and fading with an airbrush. Most of my weathering is done with a brush, but the airbrush does come in handy once in a while. The forte of an airbrush is applying evenly colored stains with feathered edges, such as soot around exhaust pipes, powder burns around gun muzzles, and grease stains with faded, indistinct edges. Light airbrushing can also be used to tone down exaggerated dry-brushing.

An often-touted use for the airbrush is for applying dust, but I find that unless the model calls for a recent, even dust coating, the effect is unrealistic. Real dust accumulates everywhere — in corners, crannies, and crevices — and is wiped or blown off exposed surfaces. That distribution can't be simulated adequately by a couple of quick passes with an airbrush.

While it is not a good "duster," an airbrush is effective for simulating faded painted surfaces, an operation that calls for a smooth and fairly transparent coat of color — not sur-

prisingly, just what airbrushes are designed for.

To weather with an airbrush, thin the paint more and set the air pressure higher than for ordinary painting. Always experiment on a piece of scrap to be sure the paint consistency and air pressure are correct before working on the model. For grease, soot, and other stains, simply mix an appropriate color and spray it on in the desired pattern. Use restraint; when airbrushing stains, a little is a lot.

Light tan and gray are the best colors for simulating faded paint, and they should be thinned even more than other colors used for weathering. Spray a light coating over all the upper surfaces of the model, including the decals, gradually building up thin coats until you achieve the desired degree of fading. Be careful not to get carried away and overdo this effect — it can't be "un-faded." Use the same method for toning down harsh dry-brushing.

Step 4: Using pastels. Pastel chalks are an artist's material which, when ground up with sandpaper, provides fine powdered color that can be applied with a brush. Many of the subtle colors and tones possible with pastels are far beyond the capabilities of an airbrush.

Pastel chalk sticks can be obtained from any art supply store. The ones you want are soft artist's pastels, not hard blackboard sticks. Pastels are usually sold in sets, and a wide range of colors is available. The most useful colors for weathering are black, white, yellow ochre, burnt sienna, raw sienna, burnt umber, and raw umber. After powdering the sticks you can easily blend the powders to make different colors and lighter and darker shades.

Grind the chalk to powder by rubbing the stick on sandpaper, then apply the powder to the model with a soft brush. Don't use an expensive brush, because stroking it across the sandpaper to pick up the chalk powder will ruin the tip. Pastels work better over matte finishes than glossy ones, be-

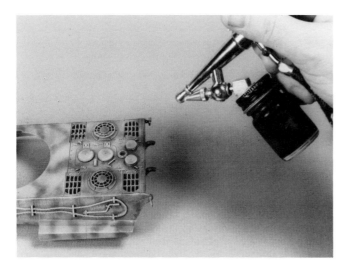

An airbrush works well for adding black exhaust stains.

Another particularly effective use of the airbrush is in applying a light coat of dust to windshields. Note the crescent of masking tape used to shield the area that would be swept by the wiper.

cause the matte surface gives the powder something to grip.

Broad strokes with a wide brush provide wide, even areas of color, while a scrubbing action gives a blotchy appearance. Using a small brush or the edge of a wide one makes narrow streaks of color that are particularly effective for simulating faint rust or dirt streaks on the side of the vehicle. Tapping a brush full of chalk against your finger a short distance from the surface gives a spattered effect. You'll be surprised and delighted at the subtle feathered edges and delicate shadings you can achieve.

Nothing simulates dust so perfectly as pastels, and nothing is so simple. Just brush the powder on, blow it around, and — because it is essentially dust itself — the chalk does the rest.

The only disadvantage of pastels is that they are not permanent. Artists working with pastels usually spray their finished work with a clear fixative, but this is unsatisfactory for models because the fixative can drastically alter the colors, particularly light ones, and make subtle effects disap-

pear altogether. Although unfixed colors will not change with age, the powder rubs off easily and shows fingerprints if you handle the model. For this reason, I apply pastels last, after the model is permanently attached to its base, so I will never have to handle the model itself again.

Modeling mud and chipped paint. Earlier I mentioned the heavy buildup of mud that is so typical of armored vehicles. This is easily simulated with a craft product called Celluclay, a papermache-like material sold in hobby and craft stores. Mix the Celluclay powder with water (for easier mixing, add a drop of detergent) and squeeze a generous dollop of Elmer's glue into the mixture.

Use a small screwdriver to spread the resulting goop generously across the undercarriage and on the hull behind the running gear of your model. Cake the inside of the drive sprocket heavily with the stuff, but use a much thinner application on the road wheels. Work the Celluclay and glue mixture with an old paintbrush until the texture looks right, then leave it to dry.

Celluclay has an excellent dried-mud texture as is, but a rougher texture can be obtained by mixing sand with it. When the Celluclay dries I paint and dry-brush it as usual, but it can also be colored by adding powdered colors or cement coloring to it during mixing.

Paint that has been chipped, as opposed to scuffed, can be modeled in a number of ways. The fastest is simply to paint tiny chips on the surface with gunmetal paint. It takes a little practice before you achieve realistic results every time, but this technique is more effective than you might think.

A more involved method requires thinking ahead. Before painting the model with the basic color, the area to be chipped must be painted silver or gunmetal. When the metallic color is dry, rubber cement or rubber masking compound is jabbed at the surface with an almost-dry brush, depositing irregular scabs of rubber over the silver paint. Then paint and weather the model as usual. The final touch is to rub off the rubber scabs, revealing the shiny chipped spots underneath.

Pastel chalks are excellent for subtle weathering effects. Rub the chalks vigorously against sandpaper to make powder, then apply the powder to the model with a soft brush.

To model a thick layer of caked mud built up on the underside of the hull I use a mixture of a diorama groundwork material called Celluclay and white glue. Paint the "mud" after it dries.

4
Reference and research

Careful research is an important aspect of intermediate and advanced armor modeling, and this factor, more than any other, sets the work of accomplished modelers apart from the rest. How deeply you want to delve into research is up to you, but most modelers find that research takes on a compulsive fascination of its own.

Researching a model can take as much time as actually building it, and

Picture books such as these are among the best sources of information for modeling. The best ones concentrate on a single vehicle or class of vehicles and provide a useful mix of manufacturer's factory photos, technical manual views, closeup detail shots, and combat pictures taken in the field.

surprisingly, can be just as much fun. There's a peculiar satisfaction in discovering the long-lost purpose of the mysterious do-whacky on the side of the whatchmacallit, even though that shred of information may make no difference whatsoever in how you build the vehicle to which the do-whacky is attached!

Most research information on armor comes from three sources: books, museums, and personal observation.

Building a useful reference library. Books are by far the most accessible and most important reference material (truly dedicated armor modelers usually have more reference books than completed models). Old-timers who began modeling in the '60s can remember when there were only a handful of books on WWII, few of which included good pictures of tanks. Today, fortunately, the situation has changed and there are many books to choose from.

The quantity of books in your library is not nearly as important as their quality. You don't need many books to have a solid core of useful reference material, and certain types of books are more useful than others.

Campaign histories, for example, are of limited value for modeling. They contain few useful illustrations, and references to specific vehicle types are

suspect, since tactical historians often make mistakes on technical matters.

I also find that broad anthology treatments (things like "All the German Vehicles of World War Two") aren't very useful because, although they are loaded with performance and production statistics, they seldom contain more than one photo of any particular vehicle. The exception is when that photo happens to be the only known shot of a particularly rare variant.

What kind of books should you look for? Photographs are by far the best source of modeling information, so the best books have lots of pictures. If you can draw on 15 or 20 clear photographs in three or four good books when you start on a modeling project, you'll know you can proceed with confidence. Photo books devoted entirely to one vehicle or family of vehicles are treasure troves of information, and a small stack of books of this kind is worth shelves full of others.

On the same plane with photo books are those with scale drawings. Although the accuracy of the drawings may vary according to who drew them, they are an invaluable aid in scaling parts and interpreting fuzzy photographs. Don't worry if the scale of the drawings is different from the scale in

A single good photo can be a treasure trove of information on weathering, battle damage, and details for modeling.

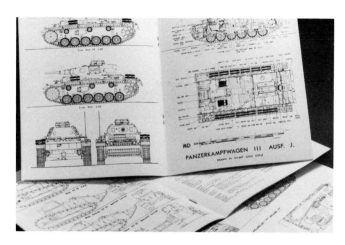

(Left) Highly detailed scale drawings are invaluable for modeling, particularly when they can be cross-checked against reference photos. (Right) Though often hard to find, interior views from technical manuals are particularly valuable, especially when modeling open-top vehicles where adding interior detail is virtually mandatory.

which you are modeling; if necessary, you can take the book to a blueprint shop and have the drawings blown up or reduced to whatever size you need.

When glancing through books at the hobby shop or bookstore, watch for interior photos. Interior shots are hard to find, and because only the most detailed books include them, they often serve as a good barometer of the value of the book as a modeling reference.

Finally, look for books with photos showing vehicles in the field. Even though factory photographs are excellent for construction details, only campaign shots show how vehicles looked in service. Campaign pictures are invaluable for weathering because they show which parts of the vehicle were most susceptible to damage. In-service views are also essential in showing the human aspect of military vehicles — how the crews lived, where and how they stowed their gear, how and where they stood and sat, and what kind of supplementary armor and other field modifications they made to the issue equipment for comfort, convenience, and safety — all important things that factory photos can never show.

Recommended research reading. Three types of books contain the most useful information for modeling.

• Modern reference books. These are technical references, many of them offered specifically for modelers, ranging from scholarly, definitive (and expensive) works like Hunnicutt's *Sherman** and Spielberger's series on German armor to the relatively inexpensive but very useful paperback photo books from Squadron/Signal.** If a book has lots of good-quality photographs, you can't go wrong.

• Technical manuals. When you can

Only campaign photos reveal exactly how vehicles looked in service, including markings (official and unofficial), extra equipment, and field modifications. Here we see road wheels, track sections, and a metal box (all held in place by a length of angle stock welded across the fenders) being used as "soft" armor on a British Sherman.

(Left) WWII Allied intelligence manuals contain a wealth of information on radio, mines, and engineer equipment often ignored by other sources. (Right) Technical manuals furnish a brand of detailing information that even picture books cannot provide.

---

* Hunnicutt, R. P., *Sherman: A History of the American Medium Tank*, Taurus Enterprises, Belmont, CA, 1978.

** Squadron/Signal Publications, 1115 Crowley Drive, Carrolton, TX 75006.

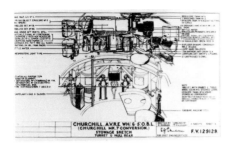

Technical manuals provide detailed information that simply cannot be found elsewhere, such as (above) the turret arrangement of a Churchill AVRE, and the propeller drive on a DD Sherman (below).

find them, these government publications are the best research material there is. Called "TMs," these pamphlets are issued to teach crews how to operate and maintain the vehicles, and they contain many photos of obscure parts that could only be of interest to a crew member or a modeler. Unfortunately, TMs are hard to find. They occasionally turn up in used bookstores, and club newsletters for AFV restoration enthusiasts (for whom these books are the bible) are full of sale and trade offers. You might also inquire at your local National Guard armory; they often have footlockers full of outdated TMs, some of which they might be persuaded to part with.

● Division histories. Most combat divisions of the U. S. Army published a combat history as a souvenir for their troops after the war. Original copies are fairly rare (check your library — it should have one or two on local units) but recently many such histories have been republished.

Understandably, the Germans didn't go in for this sort of thing immediately after the war, but in recent years an increasing number of German division histories have appeared. The photos are quite useful, even if you can't read German, and many of the German unit histories provide schematic diagrams of the equipment assigned to the units. Given the wide variety of German vehicles, some of which were issued in small numbers, division histories can be invaluable in obtaining the correct divisional markings for your models.

● Periodicals. Modeling and military history magazines are also excellent sources of information. *AFV News**, a small Canadian publication, always has interesting articles, while *Armies & Weapons*** provides good information on modern equipment. *AFV-G2**** contains excellent reference material. The English magazine *Military Modelling* often publishes armor articles, sometimes with scale drawings. The IPMS *Quarterly*, a publication of the International Plastic Modelers Society****, occasionally has some good armor articles scattered among the airplanes.

Two excellent publications that are now defunct also furnish good reference material, if you can find back issues. Profile Publications' *AFV Pro-*

Visiting an armor museum can keep you in reference material for a year. (Above) A Russian T34/85 rumbles by on July 4th at the Patton Museum at Fort Knox. (Below) Part of the "parking lot" at the Ordnance Museum at Aberdeen Proving Ground.

---

* *AFV News*, George Bradford, RR2, Preston, Ontario, Canada.

** *Armies & Weapons*, 2 Gartenstrausse, 6300 Zug, Switzerland

*** *AFV-G2*, Baron Publishing Co., ceased publication in the early 1980s.

**** IPMS/USA, P. O. Box 6369, Lincoln, NE 68506.

files and Bellona's deceptively slim *Military Vehicle Prints* contained good data, and the latter included the best armor technical drawings I've ever seen. Faded copies occasionally turn up in hobby shops.

Armor museums. Most countries have armor museums that are open to the public, and if you live nearby or can visit the area a photographic expedition to an armor museum "parking lot" can keep you in modeling reference material for years.

If you can't visit a museum in person, you can still make some use of their reference facilities by writing for information. Before you grab pencil and paper and dash off a dozen letters, however, there are several important ground rules:

1. Be courteous and allow plenty of time for a reply. Museums are invariably under-funded and understaffed, and what staffs they have are overworked. It may take them a while to get to your letter, and they are much more likely to answer an earnest and friendly letter than an imperious one.

2. Don't ask for the world. All museum staffers tell horror stories of receiving requests for "all the information you have on the Sherman"; this usually amounts to several filing cabinets. Always ask for specific information on specific production models, such as "Where were the shovels stowed on the M7B1 Priest?" or "What was the basic ammunition load for the Sherman VC Firefly?" or "Were DUKWs used in North Africa?"

3. Be prepared to pay for photographs in advance. Most museums can provide 8 x 10 prints from negatives in their files for a standard fee.

4. Use this resource sparingly. Museums should be your court of last resort, your source for reference material not available anywhere else. Don't waste a museum staffer's time asking for information that can be found in reference books in your own or a friend's library.

The two major collections of armored vehicles in the U. S. are the Ordnance Museum at Aberdeen Proving Ground, Maryland, and the Patton Museum at Fort Knox, Kentucky. Aberdeen has the older collection, containing many one-of-a-kind examples.

The Patton Museum has a growing collection and a friendly and enthusiastic staff. One of its most impressive programs is an ongoing effort to restore as many of its vehicles as possible to running condition. Every Fourth of July the old veterans are cranked up for a parade and mock battle, and each summer sees a new addition to the parade. The pride of the collection is the only operational Panther in the world.

Outside the U. S., the Royal Armoured Corps Museum in Bovington, England, has one of the world's lead-

When photographing a vehicle at a museum take lots of pictures from as many different angles as you can think of. Concentrate on details you haven't seen — or don't think you are likely to see — in picture books.

Scaling with a calculator is easy, fast, and accurate.

ing collections and reference libraries. The French museum is at Saumur, the German at Munsterlager, and the Canadian at Camp Borden, Ontario.

Visiting a museum for a reference "take." The best way to make use of a museum is to visit it with your camera. Although it always seems that the picture you really need turns out to be the one you missed, here are a few tips that will help you get the most out of your visit:

First, take plenty of film, most of it black-and-white. Few museum vehicles are in their original colors anyway, and there is no guarantee that the new colors are correct (the Patton Museum staffers still shudder at the thought of the "mad sergeant" who went around one day stenciling Afrika Korps palm trees on every German vehicle he could find). Black-and-white film and prints are less expensive than color, and often provide a clearer reference.

Shoot an overall view of the vehicle from each side, and then move in for close-ups. If the vehicle is available as a kit, concentrate on details that most kits cut corners on — periscope cages on the hatches, electrical conduits for the lights, small chains, and odd fixtures. Self-propelled guns have more stowage and mechanical detail on the gun mount than can be included in kits, so these details are worth capturing on film.

When gathering reference material for conversions or scratchbuilding, be sure to photograph everything from every conceivable angle; film is a lot cheaper than a trip back for more photos! Remember, however, that any climbing you do on the vehicles is at your own risk, and that they can be slippery devils. Many museums forbid climbing of any kind; be sure to check.

If your camera uses 120 film get standard size prints, but if you are shooting with a 35 mm camera have the film processor make contact sheets

instead of enlargements. Besides being less expensive, I find contact sheets are easier to store and use, yet large enough to show most detail, especially if you have a magnifying glass. In the rare cases when you need larger prints you can always return the negative and have enlargements made.

Personal observation. If you're at all interested in modern armor, an army post is a gold mine of information. If not, you can still learn a lot about weathering and armor vehicle operating procedures. For example, a ground guide is required to walk ahead of any tracked vehicle moving through a bivouac or garrison, and the hand signals that he uses to guide the driver (which haven't changed since WWII) are something you're not likely to learn about from a photo book!

Far and away the best places to visit are the armor training centers at Fort Knox, Kentucky, and Fort Hood, Texas, but don't ignore your local National Guard units. On the other hand, don't expect to find armor on every army post — you're not likely to see many tanks at a recruiting center or quartermaster depot.

Today's military is more sensitive than ever about its public image, and if you approach military personnel courteously and with sincere interest they will usually bend over backwards to help out if they can. The first step is to call the post public information officer to ask if the post is open to civilian visitors (if not, are there special visitors days?), what areas are restricted to military personnel, and if informal tours can be arranged for small groups. If you explain your interest clearly and honestly something can often be worked out.

Relating research to your models. On the face of it, using the reference material you have gathered would seem to be self-evident, but it takes experience to learn just what information is useful, and how much is needed.

Before starting on a specific model go through your library and photo file and pull out everything you have on the subject. If you remember seeing a kit review in a magazine, look it up; reviews often point out shortcomings of a kit, and if the turret is ten percent too small, you want to know about it ahead of time.

Study all photos carefully, making mental notes (or, if you like, a written list) of unusual features or field modifications you'd like to include in your model. At the same time, keep an eye out for small details that may be missing from the kit. Then carefully compare the kit parts to your pictures. If your reference material includes a scale drawing, run a quick check of the basic dimensions (hull, turret, gun) to make sure they are at least close.

How to work with scale drawings. Scale drawings are rarely drawn to the same scale as your model, so usually you can't lay your parts on the drawing to check them. Although you can have the drawings enlarged or reduced, doing so is expensive and time-consuming, and there is a simpler way. It involves proportional mathematics, but don't worry if you've always been a dunce at arithmetic — all you have to do is plug a few numbers into a pocket calculator, and the machine does all the work.

The key to working with scale drawings is the "scale multiplier factor," a number that expresses the proportional difference between the drawing and your model. Once you have this factor, you simply enter any dimension from the drawing into the calculator, multiply by the factor, and out comes the corresponding dimension for the model.

The first step is to determine decimal equivalents (since calculators work on decimals, not fractions) for the scale of the drawing and the scale of your model. This is done by dividing (use the calculator) the top number of the fraction by the bottom. For example,

Here's an example of using non-photographic references. Particularly in North Africa, the Germans mounted guns on all sorts of wheeled chassis. Bob Dye based his 1/35 scale model of a flak 30 on a British Chevrolet chassis on contemporary written accounts of how the field conversion was done. Chapter 6 describes a similar model.

for 1/35 scale divide 1 by 35 and the decimal equivalent is .0286 (rounded off). Decimal equivalents of common model and drawing scales are listed below.

Decimal scale equivalents:

1/35	.0286	1/76	.0132
1/32	.0312	1/72	.0139
1/24	.0417	1/48	.0208

To determine the scale multiplier factor, divide the model scale by the drawing scale. For example, suppose your model is 1/35 scale (decimal equivalent .0286) and the drawings you have are 1/24 scale (decimal equivalent .0417). Divide .0286 by .0417 and you come up with the scale multiplier factor of .6858. Multiply any measurement from the drawing by this number and the result will be the corresponding dimension for the model. Write the number down and tape it to your workbench for easy reference. If your calculator has a "constant" function (one of those buttons you thought you'd never

SCALING WITH A CALCULATOR

1. To convert a fraction scale to its decimal equivalent:
   Divide the top number in the fraction by the bottom.
2. To determine the right measurement for the model when you have the measurement of the real thing:
   Multiply the real measurement by the decimal scale equivalent of the model scale (number 1, above).
3. To determine a scale multiplier for transferring measurements from a scale drawing to your model:
   Divide the decimal equivalent of the model scale by the decimal equivalent of the drawing scale.
4. To transfer measurements from the drawing to the model:
   Multiply each drawing measurement by the scale multiplier (number 3, above).

use), entering the scale multiplier as "K" can save time.

You can even use the scale multiplier factor with drawings that don't have a stated scale. First convert a real dimension of the vehicle (overall length, for example, from a specification table) to inches (multiply by 12), then divide it by the same dimension measured off the drawing. This will give you the decimal equivalent of the scale, and you can then find the scale multiplier factor in the usual manner.

If you don't have any information on real vehicle dimensions, but know (or are willing to assume) that your model is right, you can take a dimension from the model (use millimeters; it's easier) and divide it by the same dimension on the drawing, which will give you the scale multiplier without the intermediate step. The same procedure can be used to scale measurements from photographs, but only flat-on side views can be used; there is considerable perspective distortion in even the slightest angled shots.

A scale multiplier factor can be established for any combination of two scales, and is quick and easy to use, even for beginners. Moreover, this easy mathematical method will give you scale dimensions accurate to four or more decimal places — far more accurate than a scale rule, where you have to eyeball it. Now who said your high school algebra would never come in handy?

Planning conversions and scratchbuilts. When planning a conversion make sure you have enough information to do the job; the more guesswork you have to do, the more likelihood there is of an error. If your subject is an artillery piece adapted to a vehicle chassis, for example, make sure you know exactly how it was secured to the

frame, and what modifications, if any, were made to accommodate it.

Scratchbuilding requires even more complete information. I never consider a scratchbuilding project without a decent set of scale drawings (either published or drawn myself), and as many photos as I can lay my hands on — at least half a dozen. That requirement for scale drawings is not as restrictive as it sounds; for drawings to be useful scale is more important than neatness, and they needn't show every nut, bolt, and detail. When I make my own drawings I concentrate on getting basic proportions, dimensions, and angles as accurate as possible. Other details can be scaled from the basic dimensions later, during construction.

Evaluating conflicting references. One mark of a careful researcher is that he is somewhat skeptical of all but the best sources (and suspicious of some of them, too). Just because a dimension is listed in a book or shown on a drawing does not mean it is right, especially if it conflicts with a more reliable source (such as measurements you took yourself).

The only unimpeachable source is photographs taken in the field, and on rare occasions even these are retouched for security reasons. Factory photographs often show details later modified for production, and museum displays can be altered (the best example is the Sherman "Firefly" at Aberdeen, which was mocked-up after the war to fill out the collection). There's no reason to be paranoid about it, but some healthy skepticism when faced with conflicting evidence will stand you in good stead.

A research corollary to the famous Murphy's Law states that however much information you accumulate for a given project, one key piece will always be missing. When all else fails, you must "interpolate" information.

One thing on your side is that many armor details are stock fixtures common to a variety of vehicles, things like sighting equipment, lights, tools, periscopes, and radio equipment. So, when you can't find photos of the equipment on the vehicle you are modeling, try to find the same pieces in a picture of a related contemporary vehicle. If that fails, look for information on a similar item — if you can't find photos of the Wright Cyclone engine used in the M4A1 Sherman, look for pictures of other radial engines, and hope they were not too dissimilar. Interpolation always involves calculated risk, but you'll be right more often than you're wrong.

Finally, there's the ultimate corollary of Murphy's Law as it applies to research: That elusive bit of information you gave up hope of ever finding inevitably turns up two weeks after you've finished the model!

5
Conversion and scratchbuilding techniques

Conversions and scratchbuilt models may seem a far cry from just doing a good job on an out-of-the-box kit, but in fact both involve only small extensions of the basic skills you've acquired by building kits. Once we raise the veil of mystery, advanced modeling is a good deal simpler than you might expect. Conversion and scratchbuilding consist primarily of applying a handful of basic techniques and materials to a succession of relatively simple modeling situations. This chapter describes the basic materials in detail, and tells how to use them. I'll show how to apply the techniques in the chapters that follow.

Additions to your tool kit. Every modeler gradually develops a collection of his own favorite tools. While you don't need a lot of fancy tools to advance your modeling skills, here are some items that I find useful for conversions and scratchbuilding:

• Metal straightedge and compass. The straightedge is for drawing and cutting straight lines, the compass for the same jobs for circles. Get a metal straightedge so that the knife can't damage it while cutting. The compass should be a good one, with a wheel-and-screw setting that won't change under the pressure of cutting. The compass should have interchangeable points so that one of them can be converted to a knifelike cutting edge by grinding one side flat.

• Razor saw and miter box. An extra-fine-toothed razor saw allows you to cut all materials easily, even metal, and the miter box ensures square cuts. The saw blade will dull after a while, so purchase a spare and plan on replacing the blade from time to time.

• Flush-cutting nippers. This is an item I wouldn't do without. A really good pair, often labeled "rail nippers" and found in the model railroad section of the hobby shop, is expensive for a hand tool, but can cut up to ¼"-thick styrene or brass, leaving a square end that can be dressed off with a few quick strokes of a file.

• Pin vise and drill set. A pin vise is a small modeler's hand drill. You'll need it and a set of small drills (Nos. 61-80 are often packaged and sold as a set with a stand).

• Motor tool. A hand power tool is a real time-saver when working with wood or brass. It can also be used with plastic, but you'll need a speed control accessory to slow the machine down so it won't melt plastic. Avoid those tools with built-in speed controllers — they don't slow down far enough.

• Soldering iron. Indispensable for working with brass, a soldering iron is also useful for heat-forming and texturing plastic.

An important aspect of advancing your modeling skills is learning how to use all of the many available modeling materials. Here I emphasize "all" because too many modelers work exclusively with one or two materials, ignoring the others. This approach often results in unnecessary work. Each material — styrene, wood, brass, and epoxy — has unique strengths and weaknesses, each is more suitable for some jobs than others, and each is easy to use once you know a few simple tricks of the trade.

Working with sheet styrene. Sheet styrene plastic, virtually the same material most kits are made from, is what you'll use for 90 percent of your conversions and scratchbuilding. Sheet styrene is usually white, and comes in thicknesses of 5 (.005"), 10 (.010"), 20 (.020"), 30 (.030"), 40 (.040"), and 60 (.060") thousandths of an inch. Ever-

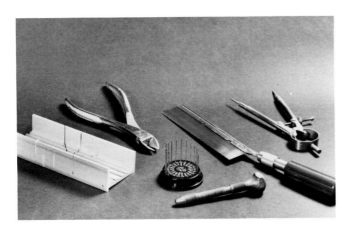
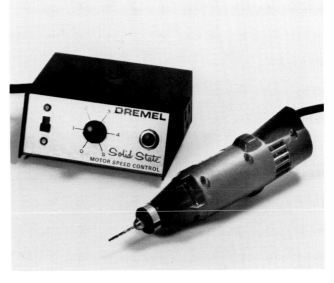

(Above) Additional hand tools for conversions and scratchbuilding. From left: miter box, flush-cutting nippers, drill set, pin vise, razor saw, and compass/dividers. A motor tool (right) can save a you a lot of time, but a speed control is essential for working with styrene because high speeds will melt plastic.

Materials for conversions and scratch-building: Evergreen plastic strips, Plastruct tubing (white), Plastruct structural shapes (dark gray), Plastic Weld (to bond ABS to styrene), and sheet styrene.

The scribe-and-snap method for cutting styrene. First score the sheet with a knife (left), then snap it apart by bending gently away from the scored line with your fingers (right).

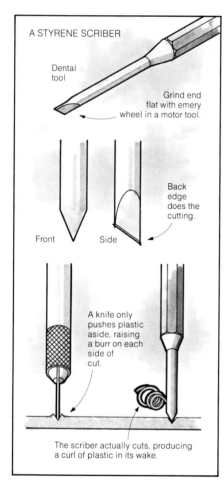

A STYRENE SCRIBER

Dental tool

Grind end flat with emery wheel in a motor tool.

Front   Side

Back edge does the cutting.

A knife only pushes plastic aside, raising a burr on each side of cut.

The scriber actually cuts, producing a curl of plastic in its wake.

Paper punches come in a variety of sizes and work well for punching neat holes in thin styrene. Both the holes and the round punch-outs are useful.

green Scale Models* makes styrene strips and scribed sheets. Small strips are not particularly useful unless you need a lot of them, since you can easily cut your own, but the thicker pieces, up to ¼" square, are useful indeed, and can save you a lot of time that would be spent laminating thinner stock.

Plastruct offers a line of ABS sheet and structural shapes that is available at most hobby shops. ABS is harder than styrene, but it is compatible if you use Plastruct's special Plastic Weld cement, which acts on both materials.

Sheet styrene is easy to cut and cement, and thin stock is flexible enough to make curved surfaces. It can be sanded and polished smooth, carved easily with a knife, and permanently formed by the application of moderate heat. Its disadvantages are that thin sections not supported from behind will gradually warp, sections thicker than the standard sheets must be laminated or constructed hollow, and small, delicate fabrications such as antennas are fragile.

Cutting sheet styrene is easy. Using a straightedge as a guide, scribe the surface once or twice with a knife, then snap the pieces apart by bending along the cut. That's all there is to it. If you do a lot of styrene work you should make a special styrene scriber from a dental tool. The scriber removes material instead of pushing it aside, eliminating the ridge raised on either side of the cut by the knife, giving you a cleaner edge. (After cutting with a knife the burr must be scraped, sanded, or shaved off.) Even curves can be cut in this manner, but thick sheets and tight curves require a couple of extra passes with the knife or scriber.

* Evergreen Scale Models, 12808 NE 125th Way, Kirkland, WA 98034.

Thin styrene can be cut with scissors or a paper cutter, and holes punched with a paper punch. Styrene strips can be cut to length with flush-cutting nippers. Styrene can be sanded using fine sandpaper wrapped around a small block of wood; cosmetic emery boards are also handy.

Sheet styrene, like the plastic in kits, is cemented with solvents that dissolve it to form permanent welds. The liquid plastic cement used to assemble kits is fine, as are a couple of industrial solvents: methyl ethyl ketone and ethylene dichloride. These solvents may be purchased by the pint or gallon from plastic supply houses or industrial or laboratory chemical distributors. They work just like standard liquid plastic cement; their big advantage is that they evaporate just a bit more quickly.

Styrene can be bonded to other materials with 5-minute epoxy or cyanoacrylate "super glue," but don't use white glue or other adhesives meant for porous surfaces such as wood; the bond may hold momentarily, but it will soon give way. Sheet styrene can be painted with the same paints used for kit models.

Because it has no grain, styrene is ideal for modeling metal, but it is also useful for modeling wood, particularly heavily weathered wood. Wood grain detail can be scribed into the surface with a scriber, or you can use the side of the point of a brand-new modeling knife blade (not the cutting edge).

The illustration on page 31 shows two simple projects you can build to gain familiarity and confidence in working with sheet styrene. Take a few minutes to try both of them (the scale isn't important — any size will do), and you'll be pleasantly surprised at

SCRIBING WOOD GRAIN IN STYRENE

When scribing, hold the knife sideways so the blade is perpendicular to the grain direction.

Note the grain lines go around knots, not through them.

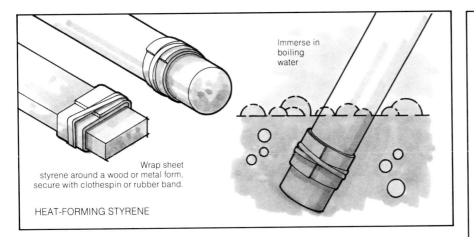

Wrap sheet
styrene around a wood or metal form,
secure with clothespin or rubber band.

Immerse in
boiling
water

HEAT-FORMING STYRENE

how quickly and easily each goes together.

Heat-forming styrene. Styrene is a thermoplastic, which means it can be formed and re-formed with heat, and there are several ways to use heat in working with it. The simplest is stretching kit sprues to make plastic rod or wire. This is done by rotating a section of sprue over a candle or other heat source until soft, then stretching to the desired thickness. Stretching hot sprue produces hair-thin wire, while allowing the plastic to cool a bit before stretching makes thicker plastic rod. Experienced sprue-stretchers will even claim that certain brands and colors of kit styrene stretch better than others!

Another simple heat-forming technique is a fast and easy way to make plastic rings, rectangular frames, and straps. It involves wrapping styrene strip around a form, holding it in place with clamps or rubber bands, and immersing it in boiling water for 5 to 10 seconds. When removed from the form the plastic will hold its shape. The form can be metal tubing or a shaped wooden block. This method can also be used with styrene sheet and stretched sprue.

More complicated shapes can be heat-formed by carving male and female die halves out of wood, clamping a piece of styrene between them, and immersing the "sandwich" in boiling water until the die halves come together. A low-temperature oven is a good substitute for the hot water, although the water is more convenient.

A variation of heat-forming, draw-forming, does require an oven. First a pattern, or form, for the desired part is carved from wood. An oversize sheet of styrene is clamped between two rectangular wooden frames and left in a warm oven until the plastic becomes soft and rubbery. The frame is then removed from the oven and quickly pulled down over the pattern before the plastic cools. When the plastic cools and hardens the form is removed, leaving an exact duplicate shape in plastic. There are severe limits on this technique as far as what shapes can be

Make styrene rod and "wire" by holding a piece of sprue over a candle until soft, then stretching it to the desired thickness.

molded, and streamlined bullet-like shapes without hollows near the center work best. I use this method most often for making gun mantlets.

Vacuum-forming. A relatively sophisticated heat-forming technique is vacuum-forming. Like draw-forming, this method involves heating a plastic sheet until it is rubbery and pulling it down over a wooden form, but the pulling action is assisted by a vacuum pump, which literally sucks the molten plastic down around the form.

A toy vacuum-former was sold some years ago by Mattel; it was perfect for modelwork, and the modelers who have one today consider themselves fortunate. Before you go out hunting down a vacuum-former, however, I should point out that while vacuum-forming is a useful technique to be aware of, it has only limited application to armor modeling. Most fabrication for scratch-built armor models can be accomplished with simpler techniques.

Modeling with wood. Wood is an excellent modeling medium when the job calls for a lot of strip material in different sizes, or when the thickness of walls or other features would make construction in plastic awkward. Its disadvantages are its visible grain (which can be eliminated, or used to advantage) and lack of strength in thin sections. Chock blocks, bridging timbers, and supplemental armor are good examples of the uses of wood in armor modeling.

Basswood is the best all-around wood

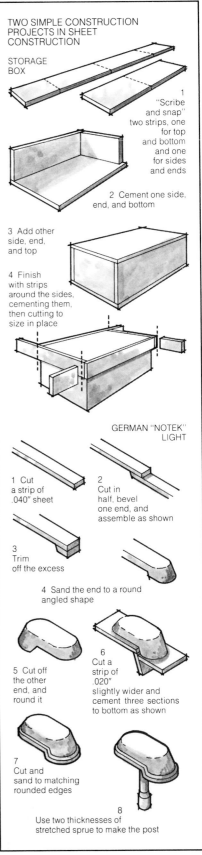

TWO SIMPLE CONSTRUCTION
PROJECTS IN SHEET
CONSTRUCTION

STORAGE
BOX

1
"Scribe
and snap"
two strips, one
for top
and bottom
and one
for sides
and ends

2 Cement one side,
end, and bottom

3 Add other
side, end,
and top

4 Finish
with strips
around the sides,
cementing them,
then cutting to
size in place

GERMAN "NOTEK"
LIGHT

1 Cut
a strip of
.040" sheet

2
Cut in
half, bevel
one end, and
assemble as shown

3
Trim
off the excess

4 Sand the end to a round
angled shape

5 Cut off
the other
end, and
round it

6
Cut a
strip of
.020"
slightly wider and
cement three sections
to bottom as shown

7
Cut and
sand to matching
rounded edges

8
Use two thicknesses of
stretched sprue to make the post

for modelbuilding; I suggest you stay away from balsa, which is too soft and flimsy for precision work. Basswood strips are available in most hobby shops in sizes ranging from $1/32$" square to $3/4$" square; structural shapes and sheet are also offered.

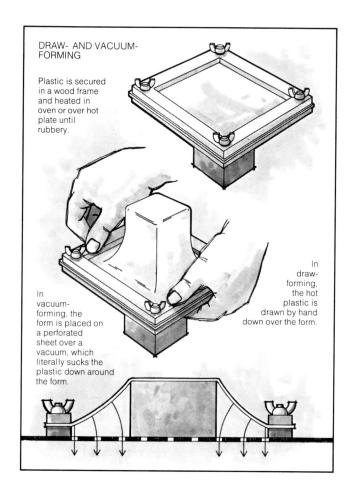

DRAW- AND VACUUM-FORMING

Plastic is secured in a wood frame and heated in oven or over hot plate until rubbery.

In vacuum-forming, the form is placed on a perforated sheet over a vacuum, which literally sucks the plastic down around the form.

In draw-forming, the hot plastic is drawn by hand down over the form.

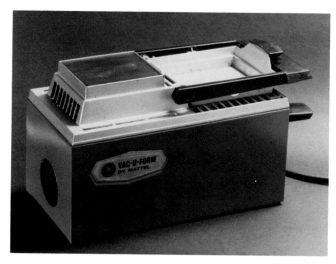

Mattell's toy Vac-U-Form is a valuable modeling tool, but it has been off the market for several years. You may find one at a garage sale, or through the classifieds in a modeling magazine.

A good example of a detail that is best made from brass wire. The sturdy guards over these lights would be next to impossible to make from sprue — and far too delicate for any handling.

The first and most important step when modeling with wood is to eliminate its natural fuzz. (Even if you can't see it, saw fuzz is there and will become visible with the first coat of paint.) Spray all wood parts with fast-drying clear lacquer to raise the grain.

When this is dry, give each piece a quick rubdown with fine steel wool. This treatment provides a smooth surface for painting, staining, or varnishing, but leaves the wood porous enough to be bonded with standard wood glues. White glues such as Elmer's Glue-All work fine, and usually don't require clamping.

Wood parts can be painted with standard modeling paints — no special preparation or priming is necessary. Wood can be stained for a variety of interesting effects. Stains accent the grain of the wood beautifully, and several excellent "weatherbeaten" stains are available in the model railroad field. Stain wood parts before assembly, because most glues are stain resistant and staining after assembly will leave ugly glue marks at all of the joints, no matter how carefully you work.

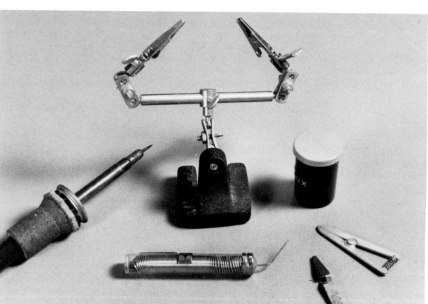

Soldering tools: soldering iron, solder, "extra hand" soldering jig, heat sinks, and flux.

Steve Zaloga made these delicate wheels for a 1/35 scale U. S. M3 halftrack by having parts photoetched in brass. The original wheels are at the top of the photo.

Making parts from brass. Brass is the ideal material when the job calls for precise curves and bends, or when you must build a delicate assembly with a lot of strength, such as a "crow's foot" radio antenna or a baggage rack. A relatively soft metal, brass can be cut with saws, snips, and nippers, can be sanded or filed smooth, and will take a high polish. When a lot of precision bending is required brass wire can be annealed (made much softer and more flexible) by heating it with a propane torch until it glows dull red, then allowing it to cool slowly. Annealing is a very useful trick to have up your sleeve — if you haven't used it yet, give it a try.

Brass can be glued with super glue or epoxy, but no glued joint will ever approach the strength of a soldered one. If you've never soldered, don't worry — miniature soldering is easy once you know how.

The tools needed are simple enough: a soldering iron, liquid soldering flux, and a fixture to hold the parts in position while soldering (the X-acto "extra-hands" device works fine). Miniature soldering is different from electrical work, because the neatness of the joint is important and requires precise control over the amount of solder applied.

Plug in the soldering iron and, while it heats up, align the parts in the holding fixture. With the work positioned and the iron hot, brush a small amount of flux onto the joint. Then cut off a small piece of solder, just enough to do the job, and pick it up with the tip of the iron. In order to get the solder to stick to the iron, you may have to clean the tip by filing or scraping away the oxide. If this doesn't work, dip only the tip of the iron into the flux.

Carry the little ball of solder to the work with the iron and touch it to the joint. Let the heat flow from the iron through the solder to the work. When the parts reach the melting temperature of the solder it will suddenly flow into the joint. Pull the iron away, let the joint cool, and you are done.

Modeling with epoxy putty. Epoxy putty is a material that few hobbyists are familiar with, since it is not commonly sold in hobby shops. It is a two-part epoxy material that comes in sticks; two equal portions of each stick are kneaded together to form a putty with the workability and consistency of modeling clay. Epoxy putty is ideal for modeling detailed shapes and compound curves that would be awkward to carve in wood or plastic.

Epoxy putty is sold for plumbing and automotive repairs, so the best places to find it are plumbing supply houses and automotive stores. The Brookstone Company* sells it by mail, and Duro E-pox-e Ribbon is widely available in dime stores.

The putty holds the exact shape it is molded into, and sets rock hard in about 2 hours. Applying low heat can reduce this time to about 15 minutes. The putty is water-soluble, sticks to itself quite well, and can be made even stickier by kneading in a bit of water.

The best tool for working the putty is one you can make yourself by painting the tip of a sharp pencil with two or three coats of gloss white Testor enamel. Instead of pushing the putty around, manipulate it by using the tool with a rolling motion. Knead the putty per the instructions, position an appropriate-sized blob of it on the model, and use the tool to gradually roll it to the correct shape.

Because it sets solid all the way through in just 2 hours, epoxy putty makes an excellent hole and seam filler, especially where thick applications are required. For filling, mix small amounts of water with the putty to make it stickier.

When set, epoxy putty can be filed, sanded, sawed, and carved. Often, putty work is best accomplished in stages: Rough out the shape with the first application of putty, smooth contours with the second, then work on final finishing with sandpaper and steel wool. This is the best way for making the flat, geometric planes required on armor models.

Casting identical parts. Long con-

---

* Brookstone Company, 127 Vose Farm Road, Peterborough, NH 03458.

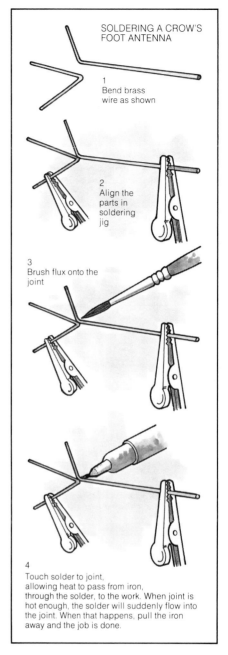

SOLDERING A CROW'S FOOT ANTENNA

1
Bend brass wire as shown

2
Align the parts in soldering jig

3
Brush flux onto the joint

4
Touch solder to joint, allowing heat to pass from iron, through the solder, to the work. When joint is hot enough, the solder will suddenly flow into the joint. When that happens, pull the iron away and the job is done.

sidered indispensable by professional modelmakers, casting is a technique that has been overlooked too long by hobbyists. It's not something you'll want to use on every model, but with the modern easy-to-use materials on

Two-part epoxy putty is a modeling material that has not received the attention it deserves from plastic modelers. There are many brands, but Biggs A + B is the one I use most often.

Epoxy putty works just like modeling clay, except that it can be sanded and filed after setting. Manipulate it with a round, pointed tool, using a rolling rather than a pushing action.

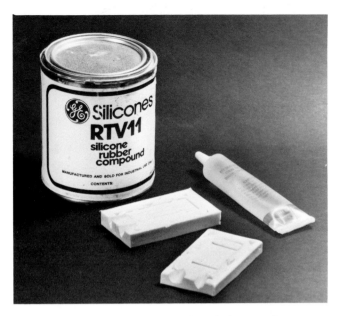

Casting your own parts is a valuable technique, and not a particularly difficult one. With the right material, shown here, even a beginner can make successful molds the first time out.

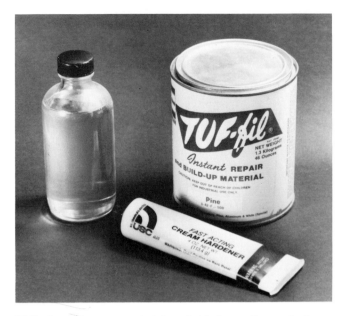

While there are many materials suitable for casting parts, I usually use a 50/50 mixture of thin clear polyester casting resin and a thick pattern-repair material called Tuf-fil.

the market there's no reason why it shouldn't be a standard part of your repertoire.

Casting is useful when you need a number of identical parts that would be difficult or time-consuming to make individually. When the parts are simple or when only two or three parts are needed, casting is rarely worth the effort. On the other hand, if the parts are difficult to make and four or more of them are needed, the time saved by casting them can be considerable. Examples of parts worth casting are hatches, access plates, wheels, radios, gun muzzles and breeches, and tools.

The first thing you need is a pattern. This can be an original kit part, a modified kit part, or scratchbuilt. If the part you wish to cast is a complex assembly you may have to break it down into subassemblies and cast each separately.

Making the mold. Molds are made from RTV (room temperature vulcanizing) rubber. The major manufacturers are General Electric and Dow Corning.* There are many types of RTV rubber for many applications; the kind you want requires no special scales for mixing, will cure against any pattern material, and is of sufficiently low viscosity to form a bubble-free mold without the use of a vacuum system. The

---

* A mail-order source for casting supplies, including RTV rubber and casting resins, is Castolite Corp., P. O. Box 391, Woodstock, IL 60098.

rubber I use is General Electric RTV 11, which comes in one-pound containers and includes a small tube of catalyst. The mixing proportions of the catalyst are not critical; the more catalyst you add, the faster the material cures. Low, humid heat can also speed curing, which normally takes from 4 to 24 hours.

You'll need to build a mold box, which serves as a dike to hold the liquid rubber until it cures. Even a crude wall of modeling clay will do the job, but the usual material is wood or styrene. The mold should surround the pattern with about $\frac{1}{2}''$ to spare on three sides and $1''$ on the fourth.

Support the pattern on a piece of bent brass wire. Insert the wire in a hole drilled in the side of the pattern, then glue the bent part of the wire to the side of the mold box with super glue, leaving the pattern suspended in midair in the center of the box.

Mix the RTV according to its directions and pour it slowly into one corner of the box until the rubber levels halfway up the side of the pattern. When this first pour of rubber has cured, use a sharp knife to cut a chunk of rubber from each corner. (When the second half is poured, these recesses will form the locking keys to keep the two halves in proper alignment.)

Coat the first half of the mold with a thin layer of Vaseline, then pour the second half, completely covering the pattern. When the second pour has cured, break open the mold, remove the pattern, and cut pouring sprues into the thick end of the mold. Cut two sprues, one to let in the resin and the other a vent to allow the air to escape as it is displaced by the resin. Make the sprues as large as possible.

Casting parts. Castings can be made

The simple wheel mold shown in the drawing on page 35, after the first half was poured.

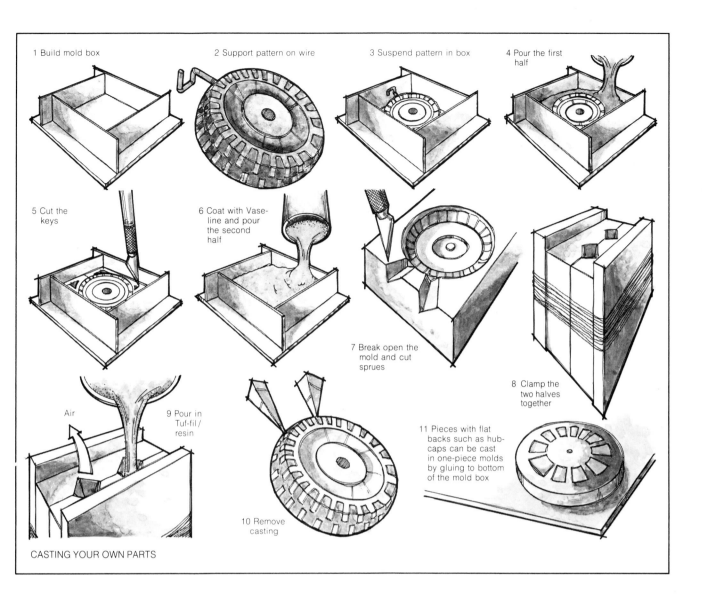

1 Build mold box

2 Support pattern on wire

3 Suspend pattern in box

4 Pour the first half

5 Cut the keys

6 Coat with Vaseline and pour the second half

7 Break open the mold and cut sprues

8 Clamp the two halves together

Air

9 Pour in Tuf-fil/resin

10 Remove casting

11 Pieces with flat backs such as hubcaps can be cast in one-piece molds by gluing to bottom of the mold box

CASTING YOUR OWN PARTS

from plaster (try Hydrocal, available at model railroad shops, or dental plaster, from a dental supply firm or scrounged from your dentist), but I recommend a 50/50 mixture of polyester resins. One ingredient is Tuf-fil,* a thick polyester patching material that is included for its fast setting time, and the other is any one of the clear polyester resins sold in craft shops for embedding things. For hardener, I use the cream hardener supplied with the Tuf-fil. Five-minute epoxy can also be used to make small detail castings, but they will be a bit rubbery and sticky when first pulled from the mold. I encourage you to experiment with all kinds of materials for casting; you'll be surprised at some of the things that work!

To cast, sandwich the mold between two blocks of wood and clamp it securely with rubber bands. Mix the Tuf-fil and resin, add the catalyst, and slowly pour the mixture into the mold, giving the air a chance to escape from the vent. One way to eliminate surface

* Tuf-fil is available from Freeman Manufacturing Co., 1152 East Broadway, Toledo, OH 43605.

air bubbles and ensure delicate surface details are filled is to brush a thin coating of resin over each of the mold halves before mating them. After filling, gently squeeze the mold with your fingers to "burp" out any large air bubbles, and leave a generous amount of resin in the sprue to replace small air bubbles as they rise to the surface.

When the resin in the sprue has cured, open the mold and remove the casting. The RTV has a tendency to inhibit the surface cure of polyester resins, so the castings may be a little sticky or have surface blemishes when they are first removed from the mold. The stickiness goes away in a day or two, and surface goo can be wiped away with acetone, nail polish remover, or liquid plastic cement.

Even if you've never tried anything like it before, this casting system is simple enough to yield good results on the first or second try. Not all of your castings will be perfect, but small air bubbles and other minor imperfections can be repaired with epoxy putty. Once you have some experience under your belt your reject rate should drop to about one casting in five.

Parts with flat, undetailed backs such as hatch covers and access plates can be cast in one-piece molds by gluing the flat surface of the master to the bottom of the mold box. The resulting one-piece open-face mold can be filled with resin, straight Tuf-fil, or 5-minute epoxy. With some parts very effective results can be obtained simply by pressing epoxy putty into the open mold cavity.

Deciding which material to use. Perhaps the most important decision in scratchbuilding a part is what material to make it from. Always choose the easiest. It may be just one material, or a combination. When faced with a new part to make I start out thinking in terms of styrene — sheet, rod, tube, or stretched sprue — and if that looks unmanageable, I think about combining styrene with brass rod or epoxy putty. Next, I consider using brass rod alone, or in combination with putty. Finally, I consider using putty alone, first in terms of shaping it entirely while it is soft, and using the technique of pre-shaping it soft and accomplishing final shaping with files after it has set.

6 Step-by-step
Two easy kit conversions

Either of these straightforward conversions would be perfect for your first "kitbash." Each involves combining two kits to make one distinctive model, yet neither requires much more work than would be required to assemble the kits without modification.

Appropriately enough, each model portrays a vehicle that was itself a conversion. During WWII the Germans mounted flak guns on chassis of all descriptions. This was particularly common in North Africa, where the practice included not only German vehicles such as the Opel and the Horch shown here, but captured equipment as well. The first model (above left) is a Tamiya 2 cm Flak 36 mounted on the Testor/Italeri Opel Maultier; the second (above right) is made by grafting the fighting compartment of an Esci Demag 1-ton half-track onto the back of a Tamiya Horch 4 x 4 truck. Both are 1/35 scale.

This reference photo for the Maultier conversion shows that relatively few changes to the vehicle are required. Note the extra wood blocks on the sides of the body.

Step-by-step instructions for the second conversion, an armed Tamiya Horch 4 x 4, begin on page 38.

The Tamiya Flak 38 gun, without the removable wheeled carriage shown here, provides the armament for the Maultier.

The first step in the Maultier conversion is to cut pieces of ⅛″ square Plastruct I beam 1″ and 2″ long and cement them to the truck bed (above left). Use the gun platform as a guide in posi-

tioning these beams. (Above right) Note that the "feet" normally used to mount the gun on the gun platform are omitted when mounting the gun on a vehicle in this manner.

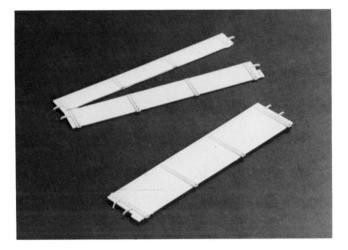

Next, modify the sides. The kit comes with an option for either high or low sides, and at first glance it might seem easier to cut the rails off the low sides than to cut the high sides in half. However, cutting the rails off the low sides leaves the lower part of the stakes still in place, and removing these and restoring the wood grain would be a messy job. Cutting down the tall sides is a simple matter of "scribe and snap."

Remove the seat supports from inside the cut-down side pieces. Use a knife, or flush-cutting nippers as shown here. Scrape the surface smooth and scribe replacement wood grain over the bare spot.

The model with one side installed and the gun cemented in place. Small styrene plates and Grandt Line nuts (see Chapter 7) have been added to secure the I beams to the bed; Grandt Line tie-rod ends have been used to fasten the gun platform to the I beams.

The extra side supports are .080″ Evergreen styrene strip (a double thickness of .040″ styrene sheet could be substituted). The edges were slightly rounded off with a knife, and here I'm drilling bolt holes with a pin vise.

The finished conversion, ready to paint.

The only reference for the Horch conversion was a fuzzy photo in an Arco book, Armored Fighting Vehicles of Germany: World War II (Duncan Crow, editor, Arco Publishing, New York, 1978). I can't reproduce it here, so the photos of my model will have to serve as your reference. This time, the gun is a Tamiya Flak 30, and once again we'll use the gun without its carriage.

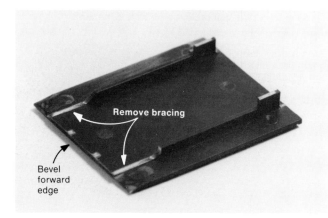

The first step in adapting the Esci Demag half-track bed is to remove some of the bracing and bevel the forward edge so it will fit snugly over the spare wheel wells on the Horch 4 x 4.

(Above) This shows how the bed fits over the spare wheel wells. Hold the bed against the vehicle side and mark the material that must be removed, then cut off the excess with nippers or by scribing and snapping (below).

(Above) Next, install the cut-down sides on the model and sand the top edges flush. Replace the doors with .020″ styrene sheet (below). Note the brace on the back of the far door (to keep it from warping), and that the top of the near door is cut intentionally oversize so it can be trimmed in place.

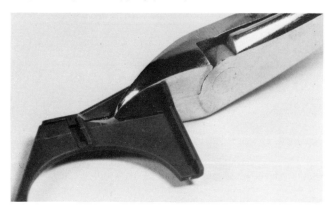

Here the half-track bed has been cemented in position, and one side rail has been propped up to aid in measuring the side extension. The small dogleg on the bottom of the extension was needed to compensate for removing too much of the side to accommodate the bed — we all make mistakes!

After adding the side extensions and back wall, cover the seams with body putty and sand smooth. It often pays to give the body a quick coat of paint to reveal flaws, then re-putty and sand again.

(Left) Remove the extended braces from the sides before adding them to the fighting compartment. Although my single reference photo did not show ammunition boxes hung on the sides, I took a calculated risk and installed them anyway, because there is no other logical storage place, except for the floor.

(Right) Wrap the windshield with tissue to improve the tarpaulin detail (see Chapter 8 on how to work with tissue).

Both photos, Bob Dye.

Bob Dye's superb Panzer IIIG includes aluminum foil fenders, air intake screening, reworked rear deck, and rebuilt drive sprockets. (Right) Painting and weathering bring out the detail.

7
Detailing and superdetailing

The term superdetailing covers a lot of ground — everything from adding a few optional items or correcting errors on a stock kit to scratchbuilt models with every nut and bolt in the right place. This aspect of modeling is what makes your model different from the same kit built by someone else.

Most modelers derive intense satisfaction from discovering details not included in a kit and adding them to their model; so much satisfaction, in fact, that experienced modelers are vaguely disappointed with a superb kit like the Italeri Panzer IV, where all they can add is one or two nuts and bolts. Secretly, many would rather have a "good old kit" that offers the challenge of adding detail upon detail, resulting in a model satisfyingly encrusted with bits of white plastic.

How to find "shortcut" materials. Here's where your imagination comes in, because many of the best superdetailing materials are those adapted for purposes other than those for which they were originally intended. The mark of a good detailer is his knack for coming up with just the right part for just the right situation.

The most obvious source for detailing parts is armor kits. For example, if your model calls for a certain type of headlight not included in the kit, you may find one in a kit of another vehicle. Most serious armor modelers keep a stock of "cannibalized" kits around just for this purpose.

Even when you can't find the exact part you need, you may be able to find something that can be adapted. For example, if the wheel you need calls for eight lug nuts, perhaps you can find one the right size with six lug nuts, shave them off, install a new set of eight, and you're ready to go. Don't

limit yourself to armor kits in one scale — 1/76 scale road wheels have all kinds of uses in 1/35 scale vehicles.

Another important source for parts is the model railroad department of your hobby shop, which carries extensive lines of plastic superdetailing parts that are ideal for armored vehicles. Air reservoirs, pumps, hydraulic lines, and other mechanical gadgets are all exquisitely detailed and cry out to be "adapted." I've been using railroad parts for years, and I still haven't the foggiest idea where most of them fit on a train!

The indispensable detailing items from the model railroad department are nut and bolt castings. These are just as common on trains as they are on tanks, and Grandt Line offers a wide variety of shapes and sizes.

Generally, the radio control section of the hobby shop is less helpful, but

Model railroad parts are ideal for armor modeling. They can be used as is, or they can be cut apart and reassembled.

Wire solder is splendid for modeling electrical wire and piping. It is extremely flexible and can be found in a variety of sizes.

Sig offers a line of small flat- and round-head copper rivets that are very handy.

Don't limit your scrounging to hobby materials, because some of the most useful gadgets are found in the most unlikely places. Keep your eyes peeled for potential goodies, whether around the house, at the grocery store, the stationer, or the florist. Often, you can pick up something on the odd hunch that it "looks miniature" and may eventually prove useful. A good example of such foraging is straight pins; they are useful for rivets, and if I see some that appear to have an odd-size head (large or small), I'll usually pick up a packet purely on speculation.

Wire solder is extremely useful. In addition to the standard sizes found in hardware and electronics stores, there are also much smaller sizes. Solder .015" in diameter is simply marvelous for modeling electrical wires, and, when braided, tow cables. Very small wire solder of this kind is usually a special-order item and the minimum order may be several pounds, but if this is divided among a group of modelers the cost is reasonable, and you'll all have enough small-diameter solder to last the rest of your modeling lives!

Correcting major kit errors. Every beginning modeler naively assumes that kits are accurate in every detail, but unfortunately that is often not the case. While major dimensional errors are not common, neither are they unheard of, and even the best manufacturers trip up occasionally.

How do you find out if dimensions are right in the first place? If you have already researched the subject and developed a "feel" for it, just looking at the kit or a partially assembled model can tip you off; if something looks wrong, there's a good chance it is. If you can, find a reliable scale drawing and compare dimensions as described in Chapter 4. One shortcut is to check reviews of the kit in back issues of modeling publications.

However you determine that a kit is inaccurate, the next step is to decide if the inaccuracy is worth fixing. To real fanatics everything is worth fixing, but for the rest of us mortals there is a point of diminishing returns where the magnitude of the error is simply not worth the effort required to correct it. If a model is .040" too short and simply adding a slab of .040" plastic will fix it, fine, but if there's a lot of detail that must be shaved off and transferred to the new surface, I'll often forget about the discrepancy.

Fixing undersize or oversize parts. When the model is too small, first check how many surface details must be removed from the problem area and later restored. If the operation looks feasible, start by removing the details. Small items such as screws, nuts, and

rivets can be carefully shaved off with a new knife blade, but larger details such as vision ports must be sawn off.

When a detail that you want to save can't be reached with a saw blade the alternative is to cut around it, leaving a ragged hole in the surface of the model (which you are going to cover anyway). Then, the excess plastic on the back of the part must be removed; a motor tool with a sanding disc or drum makes short work of this, but you can also use a knife, nippers, or a sanding block

After removing the parts you want to save, build up the surface of the model to correct the undersize dimensions. Use styrene sheet on flat or slightly curved surfaces, cementing one or several oversize sheets to the model. Allow the cement to dry thoroughly (it can take a day or two on a large area), then go back with a knife and sandpaper and trim the edges of the added sheets to size. Trimming in place is much easier and more accurate than cutting the pieces to exact size before installation; occasionally you'll have to cut pieces to fit because of blocked access to an area, but avoid doing so whenever possible.

If the undersize surface involves compound curves, such as the side of a cast turret, it can be built up with epoxy putty or plastic body putty. For thick sections epoxy putty is both more effective and easier to use. Apply the putty with your fingers, using a wet finger or round, blunt instrument to shape it. Smooth the putty as much as possible before it sets (plastic body putty can be thinned and smoothed with liquid plastic cement, acetone, or lacquer thinner). While you can always sand or file the puttied area further after it has set, leaving excess material only adds to your work.

When measurement shows a part of the vehicle is oversize, the first step is again to remove surface detail. Minor errors can then be corrected by sanding the surface down to the right dimension or contour. Start out with coarse sandpaper for maximum cutting action, then switch to medium, and then to fine to remove scratches. If you break through the surface of the plastic, sand down an additional .020" and cover the hole with a .020" sheet styrene patch. To restore curved contours add epoxy putty over the styrene patch.

Reworking incorrect angles. Angles are corrected in much the same way as inaccurate overall measurements. When the bad angle occurs at one of the natural joints of the kit, simply sand or shave the offending part to the proper angle, but be sure that doing so does not radically alter the way the parts fit together.

When the incorrect angle is molded in, the fix is more complicated. Usually, you must detach one plate, re-

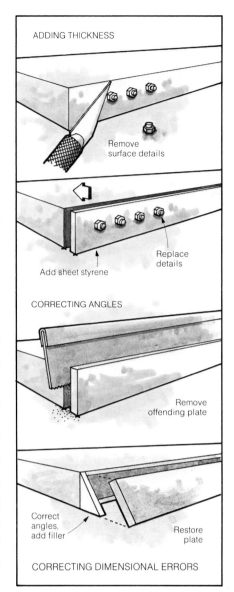

move enough material to make the angle sharper (or shim it with sheet styrene to make it less sharp), then cement the plates together again. The easiest and most efficient way to cut the plates apart is to use a thin circular saw at low speed in a motor tool, but a neat job can also be done with a razor saw. Cut close to the inside edge

Typical of a small dimensional error worth correcting is the location of the drive sprocket on the Monogram Panzer IV. It is about ¼" too far back, but easy to fix.

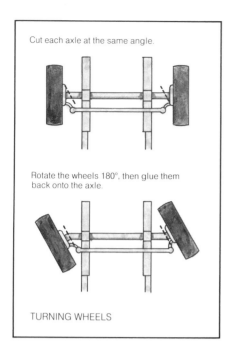

Cut each axle at the same angle.

Rotate the wheels 180°, then glue them back onto the axle.

TURNING WHEELS

Where both ends of rivets are visible, as on Jim Stephens' Mark IV gun sponson, the heads must be installed separately.

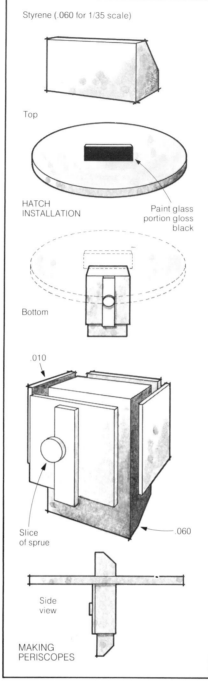

Styrene (.060 for 1/35 scale)

Top

HATCH INSTALLATION

Paint glass portion gloss black

Bottom

.010

Slice of sprue

.060

Side view

MAKING PERISCOPES

of the plate to be removed, and use a thin saw so that it removes as little plastic as possible. Otherwise, the thickness of the saw blade will throw off the width of the part as well as the angle, and you'll have to shim the joint with strips of styrene to restore the material removed.

If this discussion has discouraged you, don't worry — it was meant to. Correcting dimensional errors is such time-consuming work that only the most dedicated modelers willingly attempt it. There are a few cases when it is worth the effort, but most of the time the wiser course is either to let the errors stand and hope no one will notice (nine times out of ten, they won't), or simply to avoid kits with known major errors.

Correcting detail errors. If dimensional errors are difficult and frustrating to correct, detail errors are both easy and fun. Moreover, other modelers who have built the same kit will notice and appreciate the detail errors you've corrected, particularly if they happened to miss them themselves.

Manufacturers often omit small details, partly out of honest ignorance, but more often for technical or economic reasons. With mold costs running up to thousands of dollars per part, it's easy to understand why small details get left off. Fortunately, the omitted parts are easy to replace, and superdetailing a kit model is not a single difficult task, but rather a lot of easy tasks repeated over and over, yielding a result that looks more difficult than it is.

There are three kinds of detail errors: details molded in place that should be separate, details positioned incorrectly, and details omitted altogether. The first problem is most often found in older kits, and usually involves tools molded on the vehicle. In many cases it's wise to leave them that way, relying on the dark wash used in weathering to make them appear separate even if they are not.

The best way to remove molded-on details is with a coarse sanding disc in a motor tool, followed by hand sanding with progressively finer grades of sandpaper to remove scratches and smooth the surface. New tools or detail items scavenged from another kit or from an accessory packet are then cemented in place. When there is texture, such as safety tread on a fender, under the unwanted detail, the job is much more complicated. In such cases you have a choice of replacing the textured section behind the detail (if you can find a matching replacement) or the entire fender.

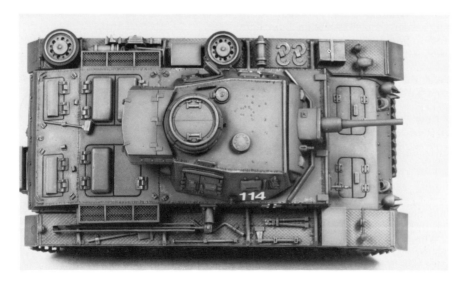

A top view of Bob Dye's PzKpfw IIIG, showing the profusion of screws on the turret roof that secured equipment inside. This is a detail most modelers overlook.

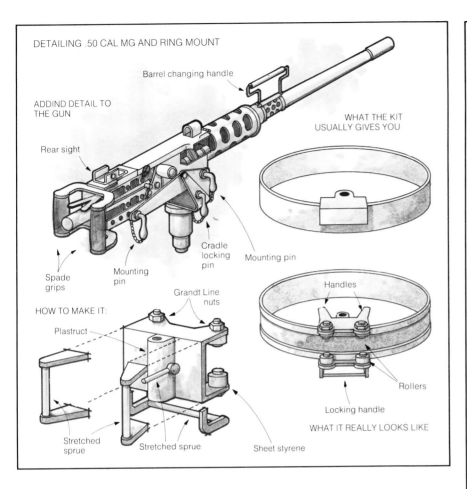

DETAILING .50 CAL MG AND RING MOUNT

Barrel changing handle

ADDIND DETAIL TO THE GUN

Rear sight

WHAT THE KIT USUALLY GIVES YOU

Spade grips

Mounting pin

Cradle locking pin

Mounting pin

HOW TO MAKE IT:

Grandt Line nuts

Plastruct

Handles

Stretched sprue

Stretched sprue

Sheet styrene

Rollers

Locking handle

WHAT IT REALLY LOOKS LIKE

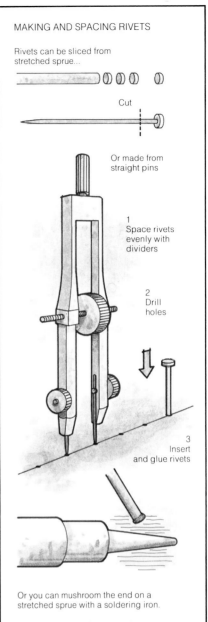

MAKING AND SPACING RIVETS

Rivets can be sliced from stretched sprue...

Cut

Or made from straight pins

1 Space rivets evenly with dividers

2 Drill holes

3 Insert and glue rivets

Or you can mushroom the end on a stretched sprue with a soldering iron.

Repositioning separate details is a good deal easier — simply cut off the locating pins and cement the part in the proper location, then fill putty, try plugging the holes with the tapered end of a piece of stretched sprue; because of the taper it will fit snugly in any size hole.

One easy-to-make detail is often missing from even the finest kits: periscopes. The brackets and mountings are always there, but for some reason the periscopes themselves are overlooked, perhaps because such optical equipment is mounted only for actual use and would not have been installed on the prototype vehicle that the kit manufacturer inspected. The drawing shows how to make periscopes from styrene strips. Paint the glass faces black, not silver, and add an olive drab or sand edge around them.

Adding nuts, screws, and rivets. Next to periscopes, the most frequently omitted details are nuts, screws, and rivets. As mentioned above, model railroad nuts and bolts are available in a wide variety of shapes and sizes, and they are easy to install. For precise positioning you can drill holes as described below for rivets, but I usually just cut the nut off flush with the shaft and cement it in the desired position.

Screws and hex-head bolts are a little harder, since they must be scrounged from other models. For example, the

sides of the old Monogram 1/32 scale U. S. half-track kit are a great source of screw heads, and I try to keep several of the kits on hand just for that feature. Similarly, the road wheels of the Tamiya 1/35 scale Panther are a good source of hex-head bolts. Using a new knife blade, carefully shave off the screws or bolt heads. Then position them on the model, touch each lightly with your cement brush, and the job is done.

Make flat-head rivets, and small rivets of all types, by cutting slices from a length of stretched sprue; make roundhead rivets by holding the end of the sprue near a soldering iron or candle to mushroom the head.

It's hard to make uniform roundhead rivets from sprue, so when you need a whole row of identical rivets, use pins or model airplane rivets. Install these by drilling a small hole through the plastic at each rivet location and inserting the pins — the shafts can be cut to length either before or after installation.

Where rivet heads will be visible on both sides of a plate, as on a gun shield, cut pin or rivet heads off their shafts and glue the heads in place with super glue; a hole will still be a big help in locating the heads precisely. Position each rivet head, touch a drop of glue to it so the glue runs underneath, and soak off the excess cement with the corner of a tissue. Excess su-

per glue can also be cleaned off with acetone.

When installing a line of rivets, bolts, or screws, don't make the mistake of thinking you can do it by eye; the result will invariably turn out crooked. Mark a line with a sharp pencil or scriber (scribe lightly, so the line can be removed later with steel wool) and use that as a guide. Mark each rivet location by setting dividers at the proper rivet spacing and "walking" them down the line, pressing the point sharply into the plastic at each step.

Machine guns and mounts. Many kit manufacturers take shortcuts with machine guns and mounts, which are often molded as one piece with important details missing. When adding details, it's important to understand how such guns are mounted. Most mounts consist of a cradle for the gun, a swivel mount, and often a counterbalance weight or spring to facilitate travers-

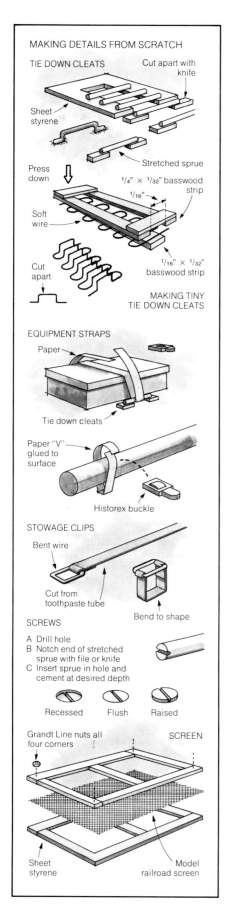

MAKING DETAILS FROM SCRATCH

TIE DOWN CLEATS

Cut apart with knife

Sheet styrene

Stretched sprue

Press down

1/4" × 1/32" basswood strip

1/16"

Soft wire

1/16" × 1/32" basswood strip

Cut apart

MAKING TINY TIE DOWN CLEATS

EQUIPMENT STRAPS

Paper

Tie down cleats

Paper "V" glued to surface

Historex buckle

STOWAGE CLIPS

Bent wire

Cut from toothpaste tube

Bend to shape

SCREWS

A Drill hole
B Notch end of stretched sprue with file or knife
C Insert sprue in hole and cement at desired depth

Recessed   Flush   Raised

Grandt Line nuts all four corners   SCREEN

Sheet styrene

Model railroad screen

Both photos, Paul Budzik.

Oscar Neubert originally made these detailed 1/32 scale machine guns for his own models, but they are now available as Cal-Scale Combat Series brass castings.

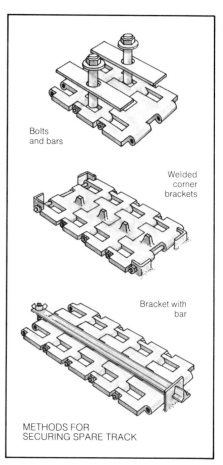

Bolts and bars

Welded corner brackets

Bracket with bar

METHODS FOR SECURING SPARE TRACK

My PzKpfw IVE was converted from the Monogram H version. Details include extensive supplemental armor, new hatch covers, open transmission hatches on the front of the hull, redesigned idler, new Notek light and headlights, and numerous smaller details.

ing and elevating. The gun is secured to the mount by a spring latch or steel retaining pins.

Whether inside or outside the vehicle hull, the guns themselves are usu-

ally blued (parkerized) steel, and are demounted and stored inside the vehicle for protection when not actually in service. The mounts, on the other hand, are permanent parts of the vehicle and are painted its basic color. The ammunition box is usually in a tray attached to the mount, not the gun, and on the march the gun is kept ready to fire with the belt locked in the feedway, a round in the chamber, and the safety on. The drawing shows de-

tails that should be added to all but the best kit machine guns.

Supplementary armor. Supplementary armor takes two forms: appliqué armor, welded or bolted to the vehicle surface; and skirt armor, spaced some distance away from the vehicle.

Appliqué armor is added at a factory or repair depot and is bolted or welded in place. This was used on certain models of the Panzer III and IV, but was most commonly seen on the Sherman, where an official modification specified that plates be welded over ammunition locations in the turret and hull to reduce vulnerability to the German "88."

Flat hull plates are easily modeled with sheet styrene, but turret plates must be curved slightly. Bend, test the fit, and bend again until a satisfactory match is obtained. If you have trouble bending appliqué plates, try making them from epoxy putty, then sanding smooth after the putty has set. To simulate the weld seam, surround each plate, flat or curved, with a thin strip of epoxy putty and texture it with the point of a scriber.

The Germans used skirt armor extensively in WWII. It was not expected to stop enemy shot, but designed to pre-detonate shaped-charge projectiles before they hit the main armor, dissipating their force enough to prevent penetration. Although photographs can give the mistaken impression that this armor was thin sheet metal hung on flimsy racks, actually the sheets were ¼" armor plate, heavy enough to require a sturdy support system. Many German vehicle kits include skirt armor purposely molded too thick (for ease of kit production), although some manufacturers have cleverly beveled the edges for a thinner appearance.

To make scale thickness replacement skirt armor, lay the skirts from the kit on a sheet of .020" styrene and cut around them (.010" is actually closer to scale thickness for 1/35, but is too prone to warp; if the thickness of the .020" bothers you, bevel the edge carefully by scraping with a knife).

If the racks in the kit are also thick and clumsy, use them as patterns to make new racks from Plastruct shapes and styrene. German side skirt armor was secured not only to the racks and brackets, but to the fenders as well, and this will give your replacement skirt assemblies the rigidity they might otherwise lack. Also note that German skirt armor was not perpendicular to the ground, but toed in at the bottom at a 10-degree angle.

Latches and fasteners. On real vehicles all tools and on-vehicle equipment are secured by special brackets or straps, but many kits omit the details of latches, straps, and fasteners that hold down these loose items. In WWII the Germans generally favored spring latches or screws with wing nuts while American practice was to use canvas straps with cinch buckles.

Handy items for modeling either type of stowage fastener are the buckles provided with Historex 54 mm figures. These can be ordered separately* (Historex also makes many other use-

* Historex parts are available from their U. S. distributor, Coulter-Bennett Ltd., 12158 Hamlin Street, North Hollywood, CA 91606

The German skirt armor in kits is often massively overscale. It's easy to replace the kit plates with sheet styrene, yielding a much better appearance. The frames can also be replaced with sheet styrene and Plastruct, as on my Monogram Stug IV.

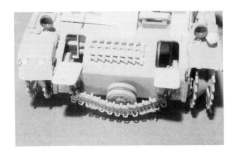

A closeup of my PzKpfw IVE shows the spare track hung on the front. The track was dipped in boiling water, then curved and the guide teeth drilled out. The transmission is visible through the hatches.

Ron Foulks

Beautifully executed external fuel tank detail on Ron Foulks' Tamiya T-62A.

ful parts that can be adapted for armor modeling and dioramas). The canvas straps used to secure U. S. equipment can be made with paper. Fold a strip of paper into a "V" shape, glue the point of the "V" to the vehicle under the part, fold and glue the straps over it, and finish it off with a Historex buckle.

Many modelers glue spare track sections to their models without stopping to think how they were actually secured. They require a bracket of some sort, often two posts welded to the armor plate and protruding through holes in the track, with a cross plate bolted between them. The drawing shows this and two other stowage arrangements; all are easily modeled with model railroad bolts and styrene strip. Tracks used purely as supplementary armor were sometimes welded in place, often crudely. Simulate the weld beads with epoxy putty.

Electrical cables and external fuel tanks. Lights and electrical equipment on the outside of the vehicle need power cables — without electricity, they don't work. Wires are sometimes hid-

den in the mounting pipe, but more often there is an external cable. For modern xenon searchlights, this cable is pretty thick (about 1"); simple headlamps require only a ¼" wire. Both types are easily modeled with wire solder.

Similarly, external fuel tanks of the type favored by the Soviet army also need connections to the vehicle. Such connections are barely visible on WWII Russian tanks, but modern vehicles like the T-62 have a fairly complex system of external plumbing leading from one tank to the next. Here again, use wire solder or soft brass wire.

Making brackets and pipe frames. The most prominent examples of fabricated metal brackets and frames on armored vehicles are the pipe-frame antennas used by the Germans on their WWII command and communications vehicles. Most kits include them, but if you are faced with the task of having to make one, don't despair. First, see if you can scrounge or adapt one from another kit. If not, make the frame from brass wire.

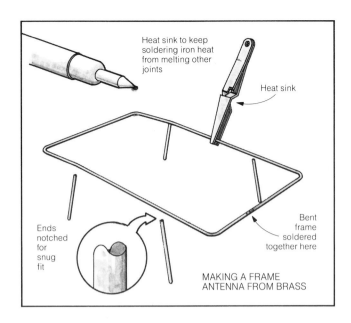

MAKING A FRAME
ANTENNA FROM BRASS

Heat sink to keep soldering iron heat from melting other joints

Heat sink

Ends notched for snug fit

Bent frame soldered together here

A typical German frame antenna on Dave Smith's Tamiya SdKfz 23l. Note how a flag has been wrapped around the frame to aid in recognition of the vehicle by friendly aircraft.

Use soft or half-hard brass wire. Cut and bend the parts to shape, and where parts join the curved surface of the wire, file a round notch in the end for a better fit. These frames can be glued together with super glue, but the assembly will be very fragile; for a durable job, the joints should be soldered. Solder the pipe frame as described in Chapter 5. Because of the multiple joints you will have to use heat sinks, small metal clamps placed on either side of the joint being soldered. Available at any electronics store, the heat sinks draw off just enough heat to prevent melting the nearby finished joints.

Modeling small mounting brackets for tools or other equipment can some-times be complicated, particularly if you want to show the brackets empty. (It's easier when the equipment is in place, because you can usually build the framework around it.) The most common examples are the brackets that hold jerry cans. Some are factory installations, others are field modifications, but all are sheet metal affairs that are hard to duplicate with styrene sheet. The key to modeling these brackets is heat-forming.

First carve and sand a block of wood to the size and shape of the jerry can — this will be your form. Wrap the form with styrene strips, clamping them in place with a clothespin (use new styrene; old styrene becomes brittle with age and may break when bent). Immerse the assembly in boiling water for about 10 seconds, remove, allow to cool, and disassemble. The frame parts should hold their new shape.

To make the base of the bracket, cement one of the formed frames to a

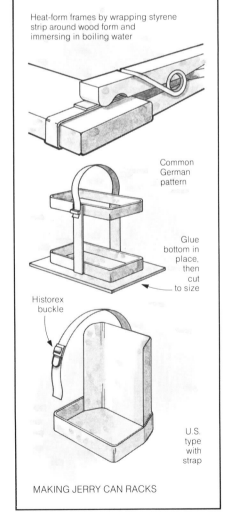

Heat-form frames by wrapping styrene strip around wood form and immersing in boiling water

Common German pattern

Glue bottom in place, then cut to size

Historex buckle

U.S. type with strap

MAKING JERRY CAN RACKS

This vehicle at Aberdeen has spare tracks hung on the edge of the fighting compartment, hollow grab handles, and typical German clip fasteners for tools.

The rear deck of my Tamiya Tiger I, showing the screening applied over the air intakes, complete with holes, and a spare road wheel hooked over the old air cleaner clamp.

sheet of .010″ styrene, then cut around it. Next, glue a vertical strip to the back, wide for U. S., narrow for German. If called for, add a second heat-formed frame at the top of the vertical strip. Finish the bracket by cementing .020″ blocks behind it to mount it to the vehicle, add a loose paper strap with a Historex buckle, and the job is done.

Modeling Zimmerit. In 1943 the Germans suffered increasing casualties from magnetic limpet mines attached to tank hulls by daring Russian infantrymen. To counter this threat, the Germans applied a special plaster or cement coating called Zimmerit to their vehicles. Zimmerit had no special anti-magnetic properties of its own, but when applied in a corrugated pattern, it acted as a nonmagnetic spacer, keeping the mines far enough from the metal surface that they would not stick. The corrugated pattern also meant that the required thickness could be built up without adding too much weight to the vehicle.

Zimmerit was applied only to those parts of a vehicle that were particularly vulnerable to limpet mines. There were no hard-and-fast rules, but these parts generally included all sides of the hull and turret, and sometimes the armor skirts. Only rarely was the coating applied to upper surfaces or sheet metal parts such as fenders or stowage bins. Zimmerit was used on all tanks and assault guns, but was rarely seen on self-propelled guns, half-tracks, or reconnaissance vehicles.

The most common Zimmerit pattern was corrugated, which was usually applied with special equipment at the factory. The corrugations were sometimes scored or crisscrossed with a putty knife for additional relief. Another pattern was the "waffle iron," usually seen on Sturmgeschuetz IIIs.

Adding Zimmerit to your models involves using putty, either plastic body putty (I often use Squadron green putty) or epoxy putty. Zimmerit should be applied as early in assembly as possible. Work only one surface of the model at a time. Apply a dab of putty, smoothing it into an even layer about $\frac{1}{32}$″ thick with a putty knife.

Texture the putty with a section of an old razor saw blade or a piece of Campbell model railroad corrugated siding. Drag the tool across the surface, jogging it sharply to the side every $\frac{1}{4}$″ to break the corrugations. The tool should barely touch the plastic under the putty, keeping the layer of putty thin and perfectly flat. With plastic body putty you can often skip spreading the putty over the surface; just apply putty in sufficient quantity across one end of the plate and use the tool to both spread and texture it in a single pass across the surface. The drawing on this page shows a special

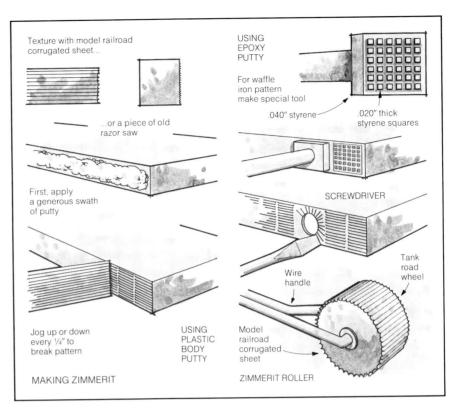

Texture with model railroad corrugated sheet...

...or a piece of old razor saw

First, apply a generous swath of putty

Jog up or down every ¼″ to break pattern

MAKING ZIMMERIT

USING PLASTIC BODY PUTTY

USING EPOXY PUTTY

For waffle iron pattern make special tool

.040″ styrene   .020″ thick styrene squares

SCREWDRIVER

Wire handle

Model railroad corrugated sheet

Tank road wheel

ZIMMERIT ROLLER

Both photos, Imperial War Museum.

(Left) The standard Zimmerit texture. Note how it has chipped off the side of the turret. (Above) A German Stug III, showing the waffle-iron Zimmerit pattern.

I applied Zimmerit to my 1/25 scale Tiger I with epoxy putty and a screwdriver. Note the changes in the pattern on the gun mantlet and around the driver's machine gun.

Three photos, Ron Foulks.

(Above) Ron Foulks made extensive use of photographs of a T-62 at Fort Knox in detailing his model. This shot shows the rough texture of the cast turret, a prominent feature many modelers overlook. (Below) The model, showing the texture achieved by bouncing a steel cutter in a motor tool across the surface. Ron also corrected the shape of the turret on the Tamiya kit, which was much too shallow.

Another view of Ron Foulks' T-62, this time showing the rebuilt lights and light cages and the weld seam on the front armor plate (also done with a motor tool and steel cutter).

tool for applying waffle-iron pattern Zimmerit.

Surface detail presents the biggest problem in applying Zimmerit. Whenever possible, apply the Zimmerit coating before separate detail parts are in place, then install them while the putty is still wet, ensuring a perfectly snug fit.

Molded-on surface detail is trickier. One solution is to carefully shave off such details, gluing them back after the Zimmerit has been applied, but this is not always practical or realistic (after all, the people working on the real vehicle had to cope with the same problem). Their solution, which works for us, too, was to apply a different pattern around surface projections such as rivets and vision ports, usually a circle or border. The most extreme example of this practice was the gun mantlet of the Sturmpanzer IV, where the Zim-

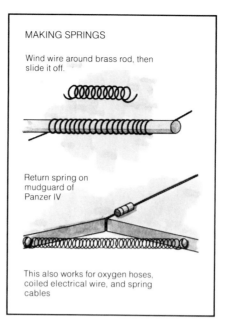

MAKING SPRINGS

Wind wire around brass rod, then slide it off.

Return spring on mudguard of Panzer IV

This also works for oxygen hoses, coiled electrical wire, and spring cables

merit pattern spread in concentric rings from the gun mantlet across the entire front plate.

For large irregular Zimmerit applications you can make a miniature roller using wire, a spare road wheel, and a strip of Campbell corrugated sheet, but for small circles and other unusual Zimmerit patterns you must form each corrugation separately, a tedious but necessary process. Here, epoxy putty is best, and the best way to texture it is by pressing a small screwdriver blade into the surface. In fact, the texturing itself goes quickly — spreading an even coat of putty around each projecting detail is what takes the time!

Ultra-superdetailing. Correcting all the minor errors and omissions in a kit model can be a lengthy job, even for an experienced and competent modeler, but there is another level of detail so minute yet so telling that its inclusion distinguishes truly superb models from those that are merely first-rate.

To include such details you must know that they exist, and this brings us back to research. However, adding this extra level of detail to a model does not necessarily require a huge stack of reference material; often, a tech manual and a handful of good photos are more than enough. What it does require is a sharp eye, and a knack for noticing the minor details that bring out the real character of the vehicle. That character consists of any (or all) of a hundred separate things, but most of them come under one of two headings: texture, and tiny (but not insignificant!) fittings.

Modeling rough surface textures. One thing that strikes you when you first see a tank close up is the smooth, crisp appearance of the rolled armor plate and sheet metal compared to the turret and other cast surfaces, which

are quite rough. The roughness is particularly characteristic of Russian vehicles. Such texture is rarely included in a kit, but when you finally see a model that does have it, you'll realize just how much was missing.

There are several ways to model rough cast surfaces. One is to spray the surface with multiple applications of liquid cement, crazing the plastic and gradually building up a soft, stippled appearance. You can heighten the effect by jabbing the wetted surface repeatedly with a stiff-bristled brush.

Another method is to mount a steel cutter in a motor tool and "bounce" the tool back and forth across the surface, creating hundreds of tiny pockmarks which can be toned down slightly with an application of liquid cement. Finally, you can apply a thin coat of plastic body putty and stipple it repeatedly with a stiff-bristled brush while it sets up. Whichever method you use, you must mask the hatch rings, periscope mounts, and any other hardware that should not have the rough cast texture. Liquid rubber mask works best for this.

Some vehicles have raised production numbers cast into the surfaces of hulls and turrets. An easy way to add these is to carefully shave the required numbers from the kit serial number on the bottom of a kit hull, glue into place, and spray with a generous coat of plastic cement to blend the numbers into the surface.

Weld seams are sometimes molded into kits, sometimes not. An easy way to simulate weld seams on flat plates is to cement the edge of a piece of .020" or .040" plastic vertically against the surface, and when it has set break it off, leaving a ragged seam. For curved surfaces apply a very thin ribbon of epoxy putty, making sure that it is straight or follows the correct contour. Texture it with a pencil point or scriber. Yet another way to simulate a weld seam is to engrave the plastic surface with a hot knife or the tip of a small soldering iron. Whatever technique you choose, practice on scrap material before working on the model.

Adding tiny fittings and details. Ultra-superdetailing includes all the little things a really good modeler is likely to pick up on — minor welding seams, electrical wiring, small return springs on fenders, locking wires on nuts and bolts, retaining pins, small chains, and even the thousands of screws that fasten small fittings to the hull. The construction methods don't differ from the techniques described throughout this chapter; extra detail is simply a matter of a lot of minor tasks repeated again and again. In the end, the degree of superdetailing you indulge in will be determined less by your skill than by the amount of time you are willing to spend on one model.

8
Modeling extra gear and equipment

An important visual aspect of any combat vehicle in the field is the profusion of bedrolls, ditty bags, and other personal gear and extra equipment hanging on it. The reason for this, of course, is that the vehicle is not only a fighting machine, but also the full-time residence of its crew members. Everything that they own must be carried with them, and with the interior already overcrowded with regulation gear, the overflow inevitably winds up being stowed outside.

In addition to their personal equipment, crew members often pick up additional spare parts, including "liberated" equipment of every description. (I've seen photographs of tanks carrying everything from bicycles to cast-iron stoves.) In his memoir, *Brazen Chariots*, Major Bob Crisp recalls how he carried an opulent brass bed on the back of his M3 "Honey" during much of the North African campaign.

If you think that you can simply let your imagination take flight when it comes to modeling extra gear and equipment, you're in for a surprise. Even here, research plays its part.

Researching stowage. The best way to learn about extra gear and stowage is, as usual, to study photographs. If you see the same item stored in the same place on several different vehicles, that must have been a pretty good place to keep it. The pins of the spare tracks on the sides of the turret, for example, seem to have been favorite stowage hangers for German Tiger crews. But remember, you can't assume something was common practice

Photo by Bob Dye.

This spare wheel on the front of Bob Dye's captured Chevrolet truck is held in place with ship model chain. Note the scratchbuilt padlock.

Both photos, U. S. Army Signal Corps.

(Left) An M8 Howitzer in action near Aachen in 1944 with a profusion of bedrolls, knapsacks, and personal gear draped all over it. Note the sandbags on the front and the black cardboard shell canisters in the foreground. (Right) Vehicle equipment runs the gamut from the necessary to the bizarre, and this Sherman crew has picked up a nice souvenir (and somebody has added a humorous touch with the GI knit cap!). Also note the use of chicken wire on the hull for securing foliage for camouflage.

U. S. half-tracks always seemed to be draped with every imaginable kind of gear, a characteristic faithfully captured in this Tamiya model by Francois Verlinden.

To make a bedroll from tissue first wet the tissue, lay it flat, fold the edges into the middle, roll up, and tie with thread.

Troops have never been above "liberating" certain items. Note the case of champagne on the back of this Monogram jeep. By the way, the large equipment box on the back of this jeep seems to have been a division-wide modification in the 11th Armored Division.

start the engine turning with a Volkswagen on cold mornings; vehicles with weak suspension components carried extra road wheels and other parts for future repairs; and American scout cars that passed through the champagne country of France were likely to have a case or two of "liberated" bubbly on hand.

Extra gear is noticeably absent in pictures of WWII Russian tanks. This reflects both the Spartan nature of the Russian army and the high expendability and casualty rates of Russian armor. Most of the war was fought on Russian soil, where looting was unthinkable, and even photos taken on the advance into Germany show little evidence of the spoils of war (the real looting was, as with every army, left to the second echelons).

Analyzing the needs of the crew. The first thing to bear in mind is that nothing was carried unless it had some practical value. Admittedly, in some cases the value might be small — a guitar or other musical instrument that one of the crew could play during lulls in the fighting is a good example — but unless the equipment served a purpose, it would be discarded.

Take a minute to analyze the needs of a typical five-man tank crew. Each crewman would have a bedroll, a ditty bag for personal items, and a duffel bag or knapsack with extra clothing. In addition, there would be two or three days' rations for each man and assorted cooking gear, both issue (tiny field stove, mess tins) and liberated (frying pan, coffee pot).

For weapons, each crewman would have a pistol belt, pistol and holster, and submachine gun. The submachine gun would be stowed in a rack inside the tank, and the pistols were rarely worn in action because the belts could snag on hatches (for this reason shoulder holsters were popular among tankers, and some armies issued them). Each crewman also had a steel helmet in addition to his tanker's helmet, and a jacket, which was never worn inside the vehicle in warm weather.

So, for a typical American five-man tank crew, we have five bedrolls (bulky sleeping bags), five ditty bags, five duffel bags, four or five cases of C-rations, five pistol belts, five steel helmets, and five tanker's jackets, all of which must be stored somewhere.

Where — and how? Unlike modelers, real tank crewmen do not enjoy the luxury of simply gluing equipment to the outside of their vehicle, and every piece of gear must be strapped, hooked, or otherwise securely fastened to the vehicle in such a way that it is not likely to be lost, even in combat. The standard storage racks are always too small, and even given the priceless ingenuity of soldiers (I was once told that there are 27 different fittings on

based on just one or two photos — just because one tank carried a circus unicycle doesn't mean they all did!

Also take into account the weather, troop morale, and any tactical and geographic factors that would affect the vehicles in the photos and the model you intend to build. Some examples: Vehicles in the desert carried far more water than those in temperate climates; German tanks operating in the Russian winter often carried a special starter coupling that allowed them to

Allied tankers tried desperate measures to counter the dreaded German "88." The log armor on the side of this Monogram Sherman is held in place with rope and mourning-veil chicken wire.

A late-WWII Sherman with heavy sandbag armor in racks on the sides and turret. Note the "grousers," extensions added to widen the tracks to spread the weight of the tank on soft ground.

the hull of an M113 personnel carrier that make great bottle openers!) the places and ways in which extra gear can be secured are limited.

There are favorite spots on every vehicle and favored items to go there. Often, regulation items are not stored where they are supposed to be — if the tank commander decides he wants to tie his bedroll where the shovel is supposed to be, who is to tell him any different?

Making bedrolls and tarpaulins. By far the most common items of equipment you'll want to install on your models will be rolled tarps, bedrolls, blankets, and sleeping bags. These are easy to make from tissue paper, and with little or no practice you'll turn them out by the dozen.

Start with a piece of facial tissue (don't use toilet paper; it dissolves in water) about 2" by 4", dip it in water, and fold the two long edges into the center. Starting at one end, roll the strip up and tie the roll with thread where the straps will go. Use long pieces of thread, then cut off the excess.

After the tissue roll has dried, add paper or card straps. Paint the rolls by first giving each a quick coat of thinner to ensure proper coverage and eliminate white spots. After the paint is thoroughly dry, dry-brush each roll and use white glue to hold it in place on the vehicle. When a roll is strapped to or suspended from something, be sure to add the straps after installing it on the vehicle, running the straps across or around the fixtures they are supposedly fastened to.

Facial tissue is excellent for duplicating all kinds of cloth: tarpaulins, discarded clothing, even drapery on figures. Wet tissue folds just like cloth, only in miniature, and the only secret of modeling cloth realistically is realizing that thin material such as a cotton shirt will have many more folds than

thick cloth such as a heavy blanket or overcoat. To simulate heavy material simply use additional layers of tissue — as many as ten plies may be required to make a thick blanket. The best way to work with several layers is to stack the tissues, cut out a rough shape, wet carefully, and then cut to the exact shape.

Drape the tarp, jacket, or blanket in place on the vehicle, carefully arranging the folds with a toothpick or paintbrush. Use dry tissues to soak off excess moisture, then brush a heavy coat of white glue over the damp tissue. After the first coat of glue dries, brush on additional coats to eliminate the telltale texture of the tissue, then paint.

Forming duffel bags. To ensure that duffel, laundry, and other soft storage bags will conform realistically to the surfaces they rest on, I usually form them right on the vehicle, from epoxy putty. Start by pressing a blob of putty onto the model, then shape it with a round, pointed tool (Chapter 5) using a rolling motion of the tool to keep the putty from sticking to it. Form wrinkles by pressing the tool into the surface of the putty, let set, and paint.

Field-applied supplementary armor. One kind of external equipment is visible evidence of the tactical situation: supplementary armor. Here we are talking not of appliqué or skirt armor installed at a repair depot, but of desperate field expedients resorted to by the troops themselves. Every army engaged in this practice, although it is most commonly seen on WWII Allied vehicles, where it represented a desperate attempt to cope with the dreaded German "88."

Spare tracks were the most common supplementary armor, and you'll find pictures of Shermans practically buried under piles of extra track sections. On models, both hard plastic tracks intended as spares and the flexible rub-

ber ones intended for the vehicle can be used to model spares. Sections lying on flat surfaces present no problem, but those that will rest on curved or angled surfaces must be bent to conform. It is easiest to use rubber track, but you can carefully immerse hard plastic sections in boiling water before bending them. Secure rubber track in place with metal pins passed through holes drilled in the hull.

Track added in the field was rarely welded or bolted in place, but be sure to position your track where it would not be likely to slide off. Whenever possible use photographs as your guide.

In addition to spare track sections, materials used to beef up Shermans and other vulnerable tanks included scrap lumber and logs. Wood plank supplementary armor can be modeled quickly from styrene or basswood. Since lumber used for this purpose would have been salvaged from wrecked buildings, stain the wood weathered gray, leaving splintered areas bright, then add chipped and peeling paint as described in Chapter 3.

Logs can be made of twigs, but be sure to search out twigs or roots with good miniature bark texture. Such wooden armor was usually secured with a jury rig of baling wire running to and from tie-down cleats, screw holes, lifting handles, and anything else that seemed likely to hold.

By the way, no tanker seriously believed that "soft" armor of this sort could stop an armor-piercing shot; at best, the added protection might slow down the projectile enough that the main armor could stop it. Like skirt armor, field-applied supplementary armor was particularly effective at predetonating the shaped charges of infantry antitank weapons, dissipating their explosive force before it reached the main armor plate.

Sandbags and sandbag racks. The most common supplementary armor of

MAKING SANDBAGS

Roll out epoxy putty and slice

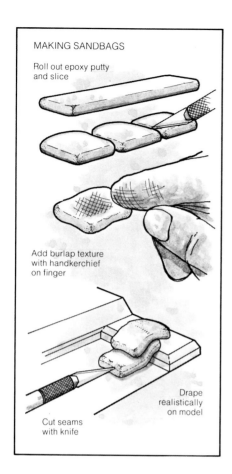

Add burlap texture with handkerchief on finger

Cut seams with knife

Drape realistically on model

RATION BOXES

Cut a block of basswood and wrap it lengthwise with index card, stained tan:

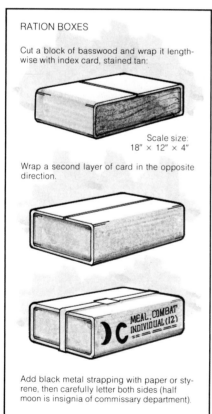

Scale size:
18″ × 12″ × 4″

Wrap a second layer of card in the opposite direction.

MEAL, COMBAT INDIVIDUAL (12)

Add black metal strapping with paper or styrene, then carefully letter both sides (half moon is insignia of commissary department).

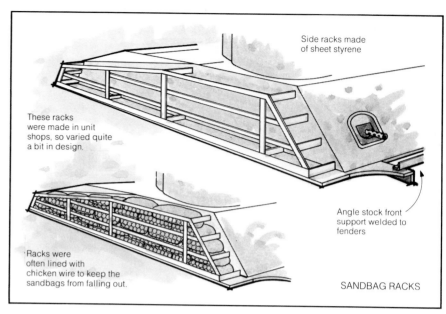

Side racks made of sheet styrene

These racks were made in unit shops, so varied quite a bit in design.

Racks were often lined with chicken wire to keep the sandbags from falling out.

Angle stock front support welded to fenders

SANDBAG RACKS

BUILDING A CRATE

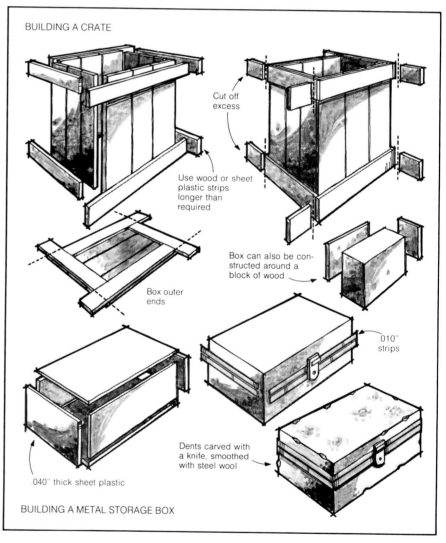

Cut off excess

Use wood or sheet plastic strips longer than required

Box outer ends

Box can also be constructed around a block of wood

.010″ strips

040″ thick sheet plastic

Dents carved with a knife, smoothed with steel wool

BUILDING A METAL STORAGE BOX

all was — and is — sandbags. In WWII great mounds of them were piled onto the fronts of tanks, and repair shops welded up sheet metal frames so sandbags could be stacked along the sides as well. In Vietnam, M48s were often encased in sandbags both in fixed defensive positions and in the field.

I prefer sandbags made from epoxy putty to those sold commercially in accessory packets because, being rigid, the molded plastic bags are difficult to fit realistically on a vehicle surface. The vibration of the vehicle, not to mention rain and small arms fire, causes real sandbags to sag and settle noticeably, and only a soft modeling material can effectively duplicate this.

To make 1/35 scale epoxy putty sandbags, roll out a length of putty about ½″ in diameter and flatten it slightly on a piece of waxed paper. Cut the roll into squares, then squeeze each with a piece of old handkerchief or shirt material to give it clothlike texture. Lay each sandbag in place on the vehicle, being careful not to smooth over the surface texture with your fingers. Then, with the bag in place, scribe a seam around the outside with a knife, and, if you wish, cut a few jagged holes to represent the effects of small arms fire. If needed, the texture on the bags can be touched up by pressing them with the cloth.

Another method for making sandbags was passed on to me by fellow modeler George Rees, who uses Chiclets chewing gum! George soaks the pieces of gum in water to dissolve the hard outer shell, leaving the soft core which can be textured as described for epoxy putty, then draped in the desired position. Once dry, the gum hardens rapidly (as anyone who has ever felt the underside of a schoolroom chair can attest!), and once painted it will not attract flies or ants. The Chiclets even come in two convenient sizes — one perfect for 1/35 scale and the other for 1/76 — so this method is particularly handy when a large number of sandbags are needed.

Sandbag racks were usually makeshift affairs. The simplest versions amounted to little more than a few metal bars welded to the hull, and can easily be modeled with Plastruct shapes or styrene strips and added to your model before installing the sandbags themselves. Elaborate racks like the one shown in the drawing on page 52 are more complicated but not much more difficult to construct. Build the frame on the vehicle, paint it, then install the sandbags layer by layer.

To duplicate chicken-wire netting inside the frame use a piece of mourning or wedding veil (being black, the mourning veil is better for modelwork). The veil material is usually available at fabric stores, hat shops, or millinery supply houses. The netting makes installation of the sandbags more difficult, but the results are worth the extra effort.

Spare parts and personal equipment. Spare vehicle parts, knapsacks, ditty bags, and other military equipment can be scavenged from armor kits. When modeling spare road wheels make sure that you include only the wheel itself, not the hub that secures it on its axle. When the hubs in the kit are separate this is not a problem, but you'll usually have to drill a hole through the center of the wheel and remove the remaining traces of the molded hub.

Frying pans, cooking pots, and the

On this Monogram Sherman note the tissue tarp covering the gear and how each item of equipment is held down to prevent its loss during passage over rough terrain.

Bedrolls, canvas, and tent poles on an SdKfz 263 converted from the Monogram kit.

In addition to the case of bubbly on the back, this jeep is loaded down with packs, bedrolls, and plenty of ration cases. Note the tire slung over the wire cutter bar.

Vehicles in North Africa always carried extra water, as on this Monogram Grant. The wood rack is made from styrene.

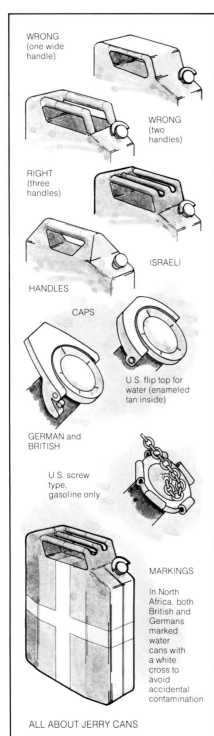

WRONG (one wide handle)

WRONG (two handles)

RIGHT (three handles)

ISRAELI

HANDLES

CAPS

U.S. flip top for water (enameled tan inside)

GERMAN and BRITISH

U.S. screw type, gasoline only

MARKINGS

In North Africa, both British and Germans marked water cans with a white cross to avoid accidental contamination

ALL ABOUT JERRY CANS

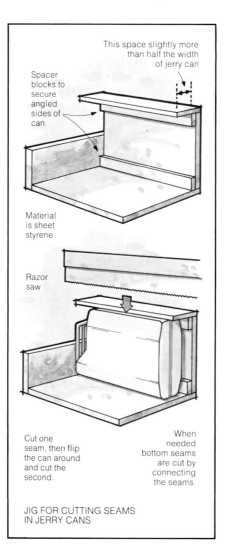

This space slightly more than half the width of jerry can

Spacer blocks to secure angled sides of can

Material is sheet styrene

Razor saw

Cut one seam, then flip the can around and cut the second.

When needed bottom seams are cut by connecting the seams.

JIG FOR CUTTING SEAMS IN JERRY CANS

like are available commercially in accessory kits for armor and military figures. Sometimes figures themselves can furnish the required items; for instance, if you want a pair of boots or overshoes hanging on the side of your tank, just cut the feet off a standing figure, hollow out the tops, and glue them to the model at a realistic angle.

Boxes and crates. There are three kinds of boxes you'll need to know how

to make: cardboard, wood, and metal. Make cardboard ration boxes by wrapping a block of wood with index card stock first in one direction, then the other. Make straps from strips of black paper, paint the half-moon commissary symbol, add a bit of faked lettering, stain the cardboard light tan, and your rations are ready.

Wood crates and metal toolboxes can be made as shown in the drawing on page 52. Note how the binding pieces at each end of the box are cut longer than necessary, glued on overlapping one another, and trimmed to length after the glue has dried. This illustrates an important modeling principle: NEVER CUT ANYTHING TO EXACT SIZE IF IT CAN BE GLUED ON OVERSIZE AND TRIMMED TO SIZE IN PLACE. This little trick will give your work the look of precise craftsmanship without any of the bother.

Metal toolboxes are best made from sheet styrene. Add handles and other hardware with bits of styrene and wire. Since such sheet metal boxes are pretty flimsy, add a few nicks and dents with a knife, file, or motor tool, rounding off the edges with fine steel wool.

Improving jerry cans. Jerry cans are important external details, but kit manufacturers often take a shortcut and mold only one or two carrying handles on the cans, instead of the standard three. To my knowledge, only the Israelis use single-handle jerry cans, so it's worthwhile to replace them with correct cans from other kits.

Another minor point of accuracy is that German jerry cans had a prominent double weld seam around their sides. This feature has been ignored by most kit manufacturers, but it's something that conscientious modelers will want to correct. However, cutting two lines so that they are centered, very close together, and parallel presents a problem. Doing it by eye is a hopeless task, and the solution to it lies in constructing a special jig to hold the saw and the can in the right positions while the cuts are made. The drawing on this page shows the jig. By laying a can in it, cutting one side, then flipping the can around to cut the other, a perfect job is possible every time.

Jigs and other assembly and cutting fixtures are real godsends whenever precise measurements or a number of identical pieces are required. Ship modelers use them all the time for making gratings, ladders, and so forth, and there is no reason such useful devices shouldn't benefit us armor modelers as well. No two jigs are alike, and each fixture must be custom designed to do a specific job or solve a unique alignment problem. My jigs often turn out to be real Rube Goldberg contraptions, but that doesn't matter — the results they make possible are what count.

9 Step-by-step
The Super Sherman

No tank in the world has had as long and active a life as the U. S. M4 Sherman. The Israeli army has been using its rebuilt Shermans for years, constantly upgrading them to keep them a match for the Soviet equipment used by their Arab adversaries.

There have been several Israeli versions of the Sherman, but the last and most powerful was the M51HV, which mounted a massive 105 mm French-built gun. Although the title "Super Sherman" is more properly applied to the predecessor of the M51, which mounted a 75 mm gun, surely this ultimate development of the legendary WWII tank is more than worthy of the name! Actually, its proper name is the "Isherman" — Israeli Sherman.

While you would be hard-pressed to accumulate enough information to model the fascinating self-propelled guns on the Sherman chassis that the Israeli Defence Force, *Zahal*, considers frontline weapons, this is not the case with the upgunned Shermans themselves, for which reference is plentiful. Here's how to model this striking vehicle in 1/35 scale, using parts from an Italeri M4A1 and a Tamiya M4A3E8.

These photos show the principal features of the M51 Isherman, including the huge 105 mm gun mounted in the old T23 turret and the counterweight added to the turret to compensate for the weight and length of the big gun. The M51 also had a new 460 hp Cummins diesel engine. Note the stowage variations on these examples.

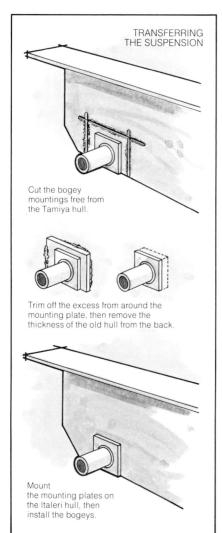

TRANSFERRING
THE SUSPENSION

Cut the bogey
mountings free from
the Tamiya hull.

Trim off the excess from around the
mounting plate, then remove the
thickness of the old hull from the back.

Mount
the mounting plates on
the Italeri hull, then
install the bogeys.

The Israelis paint their vehicles grayish-tan to make them adaptable to either the gray sand of the Golan Heights or the yellower sand of the Sinai. Whip antennas are often tied down as shown here to keep them from getting hung up on power lines or trees.

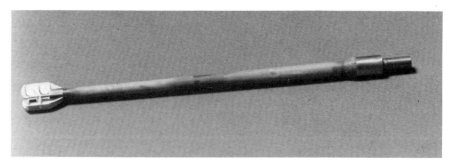

The barrel for the 105 mm gun must be scratchbuilt from brass tubing and epoxy putty.

A close-up showing the side stowage, including spare tracks, smoke grenade launchers, and the distinctive Israeli single-handle, black rubber jerry cans.

(Left) Most parts for the M51 come from the Italeri M4A1. To model the Isherman's later type HVSS suspension I used the suspension components from a Tamiya M4A3E8 Sherman. This is a good example of why it is worthwhile to scale out kits — I found that the hull and turret of the Tamiya Sherman, advertised as 1/35 scale, are actually closer to 1/32, but that the suspension is accurate for 1/35!

Start by reworking the turret. Cut a circle of .040″ styrene sheet to plug the loader's hatch, build up the back of the turret with epoxy putty, and enlarge the gun mantlet using several pieces of telescoping brass tubing. Drill holes for the new loader's hatch and file it to shape, then fill the seams around the styrene plug.

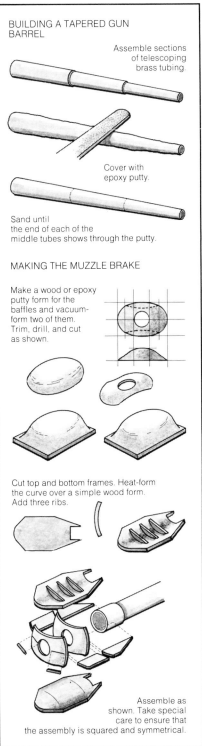

BUILDING A TAPERED GUN BARREL

Assemble sections of telescoping brass tubing.

Cover with epoxy putty.

Sand until the end of each of the middle tubes shows through the putty.

MAKING THE MUZZLE BRAKE

Make a wood or epoxy putty form for the baffles and vacuum-form two of them. Trim, drill, and cut as shown.

Cut top and bottom frames. Heat-form the curve over a simple wood form. Add three ribs.

Assemble as shown. Take special care to ensure that the assembly is squared and symmetrical.

(Left) The big 105 mm gun has an equally massive muzzle brake. I couldn't find a kit part that came close to it, so I scratchbuilt a muzzle brake from heat-formed and vacuum-formed styrene sheet. The baffles (above) were vacuum-formed, then shaped and drilled.

Extreme lighting shows the epoxy putty weld bead on the seam where the added counterweight meets the back of the Sherman turret.

(Left) The completed model before painting and weathering. The new fenders are sheet styrene with Plastruct brackets, the mantlet cover was made from tissue, and the stowage boxes were made of thick Evergreen styrene strip. The searchlight was made by covering an extra road wheel with sheet styrene, then adding a tissue cover over the front. The smoke grenade launchers on the side of the turret are brass tubing, cut in a miter box to ensure accurate square cuts.

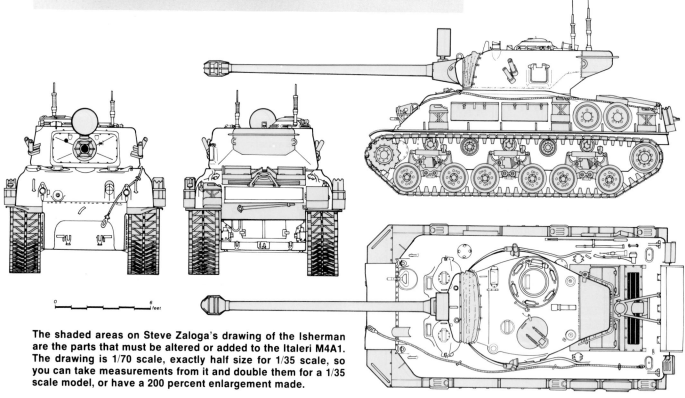

The shaded areas on Steve Zaloga's drawing of the Isherman are the parts that must be altered or added to the Italeri M4A1. The drawing is 1/70 scale, exactly half size for 1/35 scale, so you can take measurements from it and double them for a 1/35 scale model, or have a 200 percent enlargement made.

10
Battle damage

The familiar wartime image of a tank crashing into one wall of a house and out the other side is no exaggeration. An armored vehicle is designed to move through obstacles as well as over them, a tactical capability that is vital to its role as king of the battlefield. Tank crews take pleasure in hurtling their ponderous charges through the forest, effortlessly snapping limbs off larger trees and uprooting smaller ones altogether.

A tank on a battlefield is a lot like a bull in a china shop, where antisocial behavior leaves scars on the bull as well as the china. Thin sheet metal parts are bent, torn, and scraped off by buildings and trees, while armor plate surfaces are scoured by small arms fire and occasionally gouged by close calls from armor-piercing rounds. All in all, tanks take a terrific beating in combat, and any armored vehicle that has been in the field for more than a few days will bear visible evidence of wear and tear.

Modeling bent and missing sheet metal. Fenders and mudguards are relatively flimsy sheet metal, so they bend and twist easily. To model damage of this sort you must build it into the parts before assembly, because the process calls for heat and you want to be sure to distort only the areas you want, not the surrounding plastic.

To warp a fender, hold the part over a candle flame and gently prod the heated plastic with the blunt end of a pencil to determine when it becomes rubbery. After the plastic softens, use the pencil to push the plastic into the desired shape. The heat will round off the edges of the plastic, but the crispness of the edge can easily be restored by scraping it with a knife. If bending or removing a section of fender would expose a thin sheet metal edge, bevel the plastic to yield the proper appearance. Always thin the plastic after all operations that require heat are completed; otherwise the heat will cause

Jeff Decker arranged the thrown track on this tank in realistic loops, then pinned it to the base. Note how the rubber has been burned off the first three road wheels.

Bundesarchiv

Imperial War Museum

Before and after. I consider these to be two of the most unusual photos taken during WWII. (Left) A German Panzer IV of the Hitler Jugend Division on training exercises in March 1944. (Right) A photo taken by a British photographer of the same vehicle after its capture by the Allies three months later (note the white stars hastily painted on the hull). The comparison graphically shows what can happen to a tank during a brief period of active combat — for one thing, the skirt armor is missing entirely.

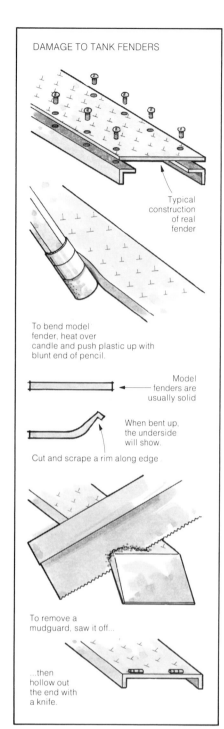

DAMAGE TO TANK FENDERS

Typical construction of real fender

To bend model fender, heat over candle and push plastic up with blunt end of pencil.

Model fenders are usually solid

When bent up, the underside will show.

Cut and scrape a rim along edge

To remove a mudguard, saw it off...

...then hollow out the end with a knife.

(Above and below) Views of my finished Panzer IVE. Photos of knocked-out tanks nearly always show all the hatches open, some left by the evacuating crew, others by enemy souvenir hunters. Rags and pieces of clothing are also usually strewn about. Careful study of these color pictures should give you many ideas not only about knocked-out tanks, but also weathering, detailing, and other aspects of armor modeling.

the thinned sections to curl back unrealistically. Whenever you bend a fender or other sheet metal part, examine your work critically to be sure that it looks bent, not melted.

Occasionally, whole sections of fender are torn off. Most often the missing sections are the separate mudguards at the front or rear of the main fender, but you'll also find reference photos where the whole fender has been ripped away. To model this, cut the desired portion from the model with a razor saw, then thin the edge of whatever remains with a knife.

Damage from enemy fire. The nonarmored portions of any armored vehicle are subject to extensive damage from high-explosive and armor-piercing rounds, and small arms fire. Jagged shrapnel holes in stowage bins are commonplace, and in some photos the

To simulate bullet holes in sheet metal, first thin the plastic part from behind with a motor tool until you can see light through it, then punch individual holes through with the tip of a knife.

Paul Decker provided this view of shrapnel damage to a Tiger I, including holes in the muffler guards and storage box.

The body panels on this VW Kubelwagen were extensively dented with a steel cutter in a motor tool, then smoothed with steel wool. The bullet hole in the windshield was drilled, and the spiderweb of cracked glass scribed in later. The slick tires were special desert issue.

A pair of shot gouges in the heavy frontal armor of a Jagdtiger at Aberdeen Proving Ground. As the firepower of WWII Allied tanks increased gouges like these were rare except on the most heavily armored vehicles.

A shot hit on the frontal armor of my 1/25 scale Tiger I. This mark was made with a steel cutter in a motor tool.

bins and boxes have been literally blown to shreds by artillery fire.

Like damaged fenders, shrapnel and bullet holes are best made before the vehicle parts are assembled. First, no matter what you've heard, don't expect to punch a bunch of holes through the plastic with a heated needle and get realistic results. The proper way to make shot-through holes is to thin out the plastic from behind with a motor tool and a steel cutter until it becomes translucent (you can see light through it), then punch and twist the holes with a knife point. Entry holes should be punched from the outside, exit holes from the inside, so that the jagged edges are bent in the right directions.

Even if the vehicle you are modeling is not to be particularly battle-scarred, it is usually good practice to add some dings and dents to the sheet metal parts. This kind of subtle damage is common even on peacetime vehicles, and it helps give these weaker structures an appearance quite different from the massive, solid look of the armor plate. Minor dings and dents are best accomplished using a round steel cutter in a motor tool. Gouge both

Small-caliber damage to the armor skirts of a Monogram Stug IV, done by punching a scriber through the sheet styrene. Note that several sections are missing altogether.

Two views of my Monogram Brumbaer before painting. Note the bent and twisted armor frames. On this model, which I built

to represent a war-weary vehicle, I chose to have the armor skirting missing altogether, a frequent occurrence.

Even shots that do penetrate are not always fatal. This German tank driver seems to have survived a particularly close call with no more than a slight head wound; note the small impact hole in the front armor plate (circled).

This sort of percussion is not what the crew had in mind when they named their vehicle "Concerto in C!" While American tankers routinely put a round into any tank they passed "to see if anyone was home" (the Germans often hid live tanks among the dead ones), this many hits on a U. S. vehicle is unusual — the Germans were too short of ammunition to waste it.

large and small dents, deep or shallow, then soften the effect by rubbing each dent vigorously with fine steel wool.

Damaged armor plate. Most battle scars on the armored portions of a vehicle are almost insignificant, consisting of gouges and small pockmarks on the surface caused by shrapnel, small arms fire, and glancing armor-piercing shots.

Although a deep gouge left by an armor-piercing shot that failed to penetrate is a nice dramatic touch, don't overdo it. Don't put more than one or two such marks on the same vehicle, and don't make a habit of adding such gouges to every tank. Most tank battles take place at relatively short ranges — where any hit is likely to be lethal — and hits that don't penetrate are the exception rather than the rule. Failure to penetrate is usually a result of one of three factors: too small a caliber gun for the armor to be penetrated (which causes relatively small gouges); firing from long range (as mentioned above, unlikely); and, most common, glancing blows which cause the round to ricochet off sloped armor or vertical plate struck at a side angle.

Direct hits, even on thick frontal armor, seldom fail to knock out even the heaviest tanks, and while you may find photos of a King Tiger with shot gouges on its front, you are not as likely to see such damage on a Sherman or Panzer IV. The best way to make shot gouges is with a steel cutter in a motor tool. Be sure to leave the plastic burr raised by the tool, since solid shot raises quite similar burrs on real armor plate.

Damaged skirt armor and frames. When I discussed construction of German skirt armor in Chapter 7 I did not mention that it was subject to extensive battle damage. These plates absorbed a lot of punishment in a fire fight, and usually showed evidence of

penetration by a variety of armor-piercing small arms and artillery. The skirts themselves were not terribly well secured to the vehicle, and thus were subject to damage from simple wear and tear as well as enemy fire.

Remember, though, that the skirts were $\frac{1}{4}$" armor plate, and armor plate doesn't bend easily. When skirt sections snagged on trees or buildings, they would be torn off the tank rather than bent. The frames that secured the skirts to the vehicle were flimsy, and missing sections of skirt were not uncommon. Many photographs of German vehicles in the field show skirt sections missing, frames twisted and bent, and the remaining skirts hanging at odd angles.

If kit-supplied skirt frames don't appear overly thick, you can retain them; otherwise, replace them with flimsier-looking ones made from Plastruct angle and sheet styrene. The frames can be heated and bent the same way as fenders, but be careful not to bend the frames so radically that none of your remaining skirt sections will fit properly.

Knocked-out and abandoned tanks. There is little difference between a knocked-out tank and an abandoned one. Whenever possible, tanks abandoned because of mechanical failure are sabotaged by the crew. Often, thermite grenades are used to burn out the engine or freeze or explode the breech block of the gun, but sometimes the crew simply drains the crankcase and lets the engine run until the cylinders freeze up.

Let's first examine how tanks are knocked out. In WWII, the most common antitank projectile was a high-velocity solid shot intended to penetrate the tank's armor and bounce around inside. Such shells create a small ragged hole at the point of impact and flake off some paint around the hole,

causing no other visible damage unless there is a secondary explosion of the tank's own ammunition.

Infantry antitank rockets and some modern antitank projectiles use shaped-charge explosives. These detonate so that their entire explosive force is concentrated on an area about the size of a coin, literally melting a hole through the armor and spraying the inside with molten metal. This, too, leaves only a small hole, but with melted rather than ragged edges.

Regardless of the type of projectile that caused it, the mark made by a fatal shot is not hard to duplicate on a model. Simply drill a relatively small hole, chip or bevel the edge, and simulate flaked or scorched paint around the hole.

The only real difficulty in modeling knocked-out tanks involves interior detail. Most photos of knocked-out tanks show all hatches open, revealing a considerable portion of the interior. Fortunately, you can logically simulate a smoke-blackened interior, greatly reducing what viewers will be able to see.

Merely adding a few items of interior stowage that can be seen through the open hatches suggests a greater level of interior detail. This will usually suffice for modeling a knocked-out vehicle. One of the most convincing details, when viewed from outside, is a few loose wires hanging from the overhead. If the engine compartment has burned the paint on the hatches will be blackened and peeling, an effect that you can duplicate easily by softening and wrinkling the paint with a little lacquer thinner, acetone, or liquid plastic cement.

When a tank burns out completely the conflagration often spreads to the rubber on the road wheels and return rollers. The rubber burns away either partially or completely, leaving just

A common feature of vehicles that have burned is that the rubber has burned off the road wheels, clearly visible on this disheveled tank. Note the bare road wheel rims and piles of light-colored ash on the track, the spare track sections that have broken loose, and the misshapen fenders and mudguards.

This is what can happen to a tank when the ammunition explodes. Wrecks like this one were common in the North African desert, where the engineers on both sides blew up all derelicts as soon as possible to deny them to the other side in the see-saw fighting that characterized that theater of the war.

the steel rims of the wheels. On a model the rubber portions can be removed by turning down the wheels in a motor tool.

Wheels and rollers that have holes in the center can be mounted on a sanding disc mandrel; otherwise, bond them to a disc of wood or plastic with super glue, then mount the disc on the mandrel. When sanding wheels keep the motor tool on low speed so the plastic doesn't melt from friction. To remove the wheel from the disc after sanding, soften the super glue with acetone or nail polish remover.

Modeling thrown track. A common armored vehicle breakdown is throwing a track, either as a result of combat damage or regular wear and tear. Most track consists of individual links connected by pins, and while the vehicle will sometimes come to a stop immediately when a pin breaks, more often it continues until it runs out of track. On firm ground the tank may continue even further, slewing sharply toward the damaged side before it grinds to a halt. When modeling a thrown track, then, you are justified in showing no track at all, part of a track, or the whole thing.

The tracks of 1/24 scale vehicles are easiest to work with, since they usually have individual links. Rubbery "loop" track is harder to control. First, make sure that your track is fully detailed on both sides, since both sides will be visible. With your vehicle in place on its base (it would be difficult indeed to model a thrown track without a base for the model), position the track and secure each end with small pins. I use insect mounting pins that have tiny heads. Drill holes in the base slightly smaller than the pins so that the pins are a force fit. Pin down each loop of track until you have the desired effect.

Demolished vehicles. Modeling a

tank that has exploded presents a real modeling challenge. Minor explosions usually do little more than lift the turret out of its ring, leaving it at a cockeyed angle, which is not hard to model and visually effective. Major explosions crack and buckle the armor plate (remember, armor plate does not bend) and occasionally pop open weld seams. The best way to simulate such catastrophic damage is to scribe the desired cracks on the back side of the armor plate, then give the model parts a good whack with a hammer.

Finally, let me add one note of cau-

tion in modeling battle damage. The catastrophic destruction caused by a major explosion will reveal the interior, which, even though the detail is to be twisted and charred, will require a lot of time and effort to model. There is a lot of wiring and equipment inside a tank, and you will have to include all of it. If the job is to be done right a shattered hulk is not a destruction job at all, but a difficult and exacting construction project involving extensive scratchbuilding. Don't try it until you are ready for it, but when you are, good luck!

Modeling an exploded vehicle requires a major modeling effort, and you would be hard-pressed to top the job done on this 1/76 scale T-34 by Steve Zaloga. Particularly noteworthy are the burned rubber on the road wheels, the bent and twisted sheet metal (one fuel tank has clearly exploded), the rear armor plate that has popped loose, and the detailed chaos of the exposed engine compartment.

11
Building from scratch

Exactly when an extensively converted armor model becomes "scratchbuilt" is difficult to define. The standard definition of scratchbuilt — built entirely from raw materials — is not much help, since most armor models accepted as scratchbuilt utilize parts scavenged from kits. I think it's reasonable to call a model scratchbuilt if the basic superstructure and hull are built from raw materials. This definition clearly distinguishes such models from converted kits, yet leaves us free to use available detail parts.

Research for scratchbuilding. Building a model from scratch calls for a lot more research material than assembling a kit. In addition to the usual assortment of photos (more than the usual assortment, if possible), the most important reference in constructing a hull and turret from scratch is accurate drawings. Check the reliability of all drawings by comparing them to photos and by making sure that the dimensions shown on the different views correspond to dimensions listed in other sources, and match each other (you'd be surprised how often side and front view drawings don't quite agree with each other).

If you can't find reliable drawings, you'll have to make your own. This is not as complicated as it sounds, since all you need to draw are basic structures — details can be simplified or omitted. Because the drawings are strictly for your own use, they needn't be particularly neat — accuracy is what counts. I use tracing paper with a light blue engineering grid, which allows me to lay one sheet on top of another to transfer or correct measurements. The grid helps in measuring, as well as ensuring that right angles are drawn accurately. For drawing, I use a sharp No. 2 pencil — with an eraser!

It's important that your working drawings be in the same scale as your model, and that you carefully work out all basic dimensions and angles before beginning construction. This allows you to use the drawings as templates, transferring all measurements directly from them to the model and checking parts for accuracy by laying them on the plan.

Basic hull and turret construction. Hulls and turrets are easy to construct from sheet styrene. While .020″ sheet is sufficiently thick not to warp in 1/76 scale, .040″ is best for 1/35. You can also use .040″ for 1/25 scale models, but broad sections will require bracing from behind.

Start by cutting a separate piece of plastic for each flat plate on the vehicle. The easiest sequence is to start with the bottom of the hull and work up. When measuring and cutting parts, be sure to allow for the thickness of the plastic.

Square parts can be laid out accurately by transferring measurements from the drawing with a ruler and triangle, but parts with complex angles are better handled by tracing from the drawing, cutting out a pattern, and drawing around the pattern to mark the plastic. Angled plates are tricky because the angles are distorted in side and end elevation drawings, so you must take only the top and bottom dimensions from the side view and the end dimensions from a top or end view.

You'll also find that angled plates are tricky to fit, because the edges

---

BASIC HULL CONSTRUCTION

Use sheet styrene, .040″ for 1/35 and larger, .020″ for smaller.

Overlapping joints

Extra bulkhead for strength

Start with bottom plate and work up.

Install plates with square-cut edges whenever possible, then sand the bevel.

Bill Stephens

Scratchbuilt models can be made in all scales and of all sorts of vehicles. (Left) A 1/25 scale Italian self-propelled gun by Jim

Steve Zaloga

Stephens. (Right) A tiny 1/76 scale Japanese amphibious tank with detachable front and rear pontoons by Steve Zaloga.

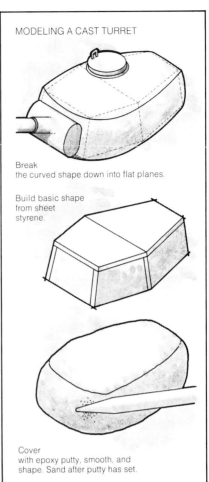

MODELING A CAST TURRET

Break
the curved shape down into flat planes.

Build basic shape
from sheet
styrene.

Cover
with epoxy putty, smooth, and
shape. Sand after putty has set.

(Above and right) The Tamiya 1/25 scale Tiger I kit contains a rudimentary interior that provides all the major elements, but about three-quarters of the detail on my model had to be built from scratch. So that all this work can be appreciated, the tank is designed to peel apart in layers, like an onion, revealing more of the interior as each layer is removed.

must be beveled. Where angled plates meet angled plates, as on the German Panther, beveling all the mating sides gets complicated. Instead of beveling each piece before assembly, I often leave some of the edges square, beveling them later, in place. Remember, too, that angles inside the hull need not be precise, as long as no visible gaps are created at the outside of the joint.

It is possible to cut out all parts before starting assembly, but I don't recommend it. I prefer to cut each part (or pair of parts, when they are identical) and install as I go. That way, if a part doesn't fit, I know right away and can make immediate adjustments. Nothing is lost when you make a part that doesn't fit; just figure out the reason for the error and cut another one.

Bracing, subassemblies, and modeling curved surfaces. Most models require at least some internal bulkheads and bracing to prevent warping. There is no precise rule of thumb to tell you when or how much reinforcement is needed; if the model gives when squeezed gently, it probably needs more bracing.

If you plan to add full interior detail, consider building the hull in several subassemblies for ease of access while installing the interior. Detailing the inside of a 1/76 scale hull by reaching through the turret hole can be a frustrating experience — just because a surgeon can tie a square knot inside a matchbox doesn't mean that you can!

To model the curved surface of a cast hull or turret start with a form built of flat plates, just as you would for a slab-sided vehicle. On paper, reduce the curved contours to flat planes, making sure none of them project beyond the

final curved surface contours. Use this drawing as a guide for construction of the model, which will purposely be too small. After assembling the form from flat sheet parts, apply epoxy putty over it and use a round, blunt tool to roll and shape the putty to the correct contours.

This plate-and-putty method won't work for models where you plan to install an interior because the flat plates, invisible from the outside, will interfere with the interior details. One solution is to vacuum-form a thin plastic shell over a built-up epoxy pattern. For complex forms such as a cast turret the epoxy pattern often must be cut in half horizontally so the top and bottom can be vacuum-formed separately. Then the two plastic shells are joined to make the finished part.

Scratchbuilding suspension components. If the vehicle you are modeling uses a standard suspension you may be able to transfer the running gear intact from a kit. If not, you will have to make the suspension, or at least parts of it, yourself. This is easier than it sounds, once you break the suspension down into its component parts: drive sprockets, idlers, road wheels (sometimes mounted on frames), return rollers, and tracks.

Whenever possible, try to cannibalize kit suspension parts. You'll be surprised how often a drive sprocket from a German vehicle can be modified and re-detailed to fit on a French tank. Drive sprockets are by far the most difficult suspension components to make from scratch. Not only must the diam-

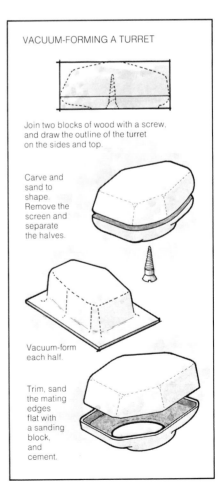

VACUUM-FORMING A TURRET

Join two blocks of wood with a screw, and draw the outline of the turret on the sides and top.

Carve and sand to shape. Remove the screen and separate the halves.

Vacuum-form each half.

Trim, sand the mating edges flat with a sanding block, and cement.

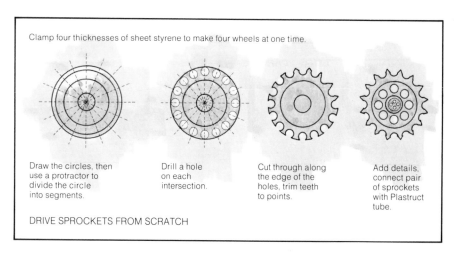

Clamp four thicknesses of sheet styrene to make four wheels at one time.

Draw the circles, then use a protractor to divide the circle into segments.

Drill a hole on each intersection.

Cut through along the edge of the holes, trim teeth to points.

Add details, connect pair of sprockets with Plastruct tube.

DRIVE SPROCKETS FROM SCRATCH

eter and detailing be right, but the number and spacing of the sprocket teeth must match the prototype and, equally important, the tracks you are going to use.

The drawing shows the steps in making drive sprockets from scratch. First use a circle template or compass to draw the required rings on sheet styrene. Divide 360° by the number of teeth on the sprocket to determine the angle between each pair of teeth. Use a protractor to mark this angular spacing around half of the outer ring, then draw lines from these points through the center to mark off the other half of the circle.

Use a drill the size of the gap between the sprocket teeth to drill a hole on each line just inside the outer ring. Next, use a circle template and scriber or a sharpened compass to cut the sprocket blanks out of the sheet. Finish the sprocket wheels by shaping the teeth and adding bolts and other surface detail.

Idler wheels with teeth can be made in the same way as drive sprockets. Smooth idlers, return rollers, and road wheels can almost always be adapted from kits. (The only alternative is to turn them on a lathe, so you'd better find a way to scavenge them somewhere!)

Wheels that are otherwise satisfactory but slightly oversize or undersize can be enlarged or reduced. To reduce the diameter mount the wheel in a motor tool, run it at low speed and sand it down with an emery board. To enlarge a wheel add one or more bands of .010" sheet styrene around the outer edge. Wheels that are too wide or too narrow can be corrected the same way; make the correction on the inner side of the wheel so that it will not show.

Building the suspension frames that mount the road wheels presents a problem not because the frames are difficult to fabricate (they can be made from styrene, stretched sprue, epoxy putty, model railroad bolts, and other standard materials), but because building six or more of them is tedious. The solution is to make one really good one as a pattern, then cast as many as you need following the techniques in Chapter 5.

Making or modifying tracks. Tracks present a similar problem, and again the best solution is to cannibalize from kits if at all possible. Kit tracks will rarely be the right length for a scratch-built model, and the drawing on this page shows how to shorten or lengthen them.

The key to scratchbuilding track lies in making one good pattern and casting as many sections as you need from it. Use sheet styrene to make a section three or four links long, double-checking that both ends are perfectly square. A slight error here can come back to haunt you, for when you assemble the cast sections end to end even the slightest angle will cause the track to gradually curve to one side or the other, making it impossible to install on the vehicle.

Make a mold from the pattern and cast two or three track sections in it, then join them to make a longer section and make another mold from it. For 1/76 scale models the entire track length is short enough to cast in one mold, if you want.

The Tuf-fil resin mixture described in Chapter 5 is sufficiently rubbery when it first comes out of the mold to bend around the suspension. If you prefer rubber track, it is possible to cast the track sections from the same RTV rubber compound used to make the molds (just be sure to coat the mold with Vaseline so it won't stick). The difficulty with RTV is in connecting the track sections, since about the only thing that will stick to RTV rubber is RTV rubber.

If you choose RTV tracks, you'll either have to staple the sections together (unsightly at best) or bond them with RTV, which is not 100 percent reliable. To do so, overlap several links, clean the area with acetone or liquid plastic cement, butter the joint with freshly mixed RTV, and clamp with a clothespin. After curing overnight the joint should hold, provided the track tension is not too great.

Building the main gun. Here again, always cannibalize if possible. If you must scratchbuild a main gun and don't have a lathe to turn the tapered barrel, an easy way is to use several lengths of telescoping brass tubing, which can usually be found in the model airplane section of your hobby shop.

The tubing with the smallest diameter should be the size of the narrow end of the barrel and the largest tube should be the size of the breech end. Space the intermediate sections so a straightedge touching both ends also touches each piece of tubing in between. Glue the tubing sections together, then cover the assembly with epoxy putty.

After the putty has set sand the barrel, starting with coarse paper for maximum cutting action, then shifting to a fine grit for final shaping. I use a sanding disc in a motor tool, rotating the barrel rapidly with my fingers to make the surface as round as possible. Check the barrel frequently with a straightedge, and sand until a thin band of brass shows through the putty at the end of each tubing section. The result may not be quite as perfect as a barrel turned on a lathe, but it looks just as good to the eye.

Interior detailing. Just how much interior detail is enough is a matter of personal modeling philosophy. I am firmly of the mind that modeling anything that can't be seen is a waste of time. While there's nothing wrong with modeling hidden detail if you derive great satisfaction just from knowing that it's there, you should be aware that that's all the satisfaction you're likely to derive from it!

When I model a vehicle with the hatches closed I don't worry about the interior at all, and if hatches will be

SHORTENING TRACK

Cut off the desired number of links.

Use a fresh blade to carefully cut the new end in half lengthwise.

Drill new holes.

The amount of detail that can be seen through open hatches is limited, so unless there is some way to open a model, effort can be wasted on interior details that will never be seen.

My Pz IVE has a partial interior. The detail had to appear complete because many hatches would be open, but the greatly restricted view meant that minor details and equipment could be suggested rather than modeled bolt-for-bolt. Many parts were scavenged from car kits — note their chrome-plated finish.

open, I model only what can be seen through those hatches. I won't attempt a fully detailed interior unless I know that there is some way I can show it off, either by opening a lot of hatches or by taking the model apart.

The amount of research material you need depends on the amount of interior detail you intend to add. A partial interior can be worked up using only one or two photos, but a full interior requires at least a dozen photographs, and cutaway or cross-section drawings, if available. If you decide to model a full-blown interior, make sure you have enough information before you start. The time to discover that you have no information on the back wall of the turret is beforehand, not when you have the interior half completed.

Partial interiors. A partial interior is the kind that is meant to be viewed through one or two open hatches. It is important to suggest detail, without going to the bother of putting in a lot of things that will never be seen. Some prominent details must be modeled accurately, including major assemblies such as the gun breech, seats, steering wheel, and instrument panel, but minor "supporting" details can be faked to varying degrees, depending upon how clearly they can be seen. Turret wall stowage, for example, can be suggested convincingly with strategically placed styrene blocks and cylinders, wire solder cables, and a few nondescript model railroad parts.

This kind of shortcut is not an excuse to "imagineer" the whole interior, and whenever possible you should use reference photos as a guide in placing "suggestive" details. The major assemblies will have to be cannibalized from kits or scratchbuilt.

Full interior detail. Any model with complete interior detail is an ambitious undertaking. Still, the work required is within the capabilities of any modeler with several kits under his belt. In fact, the Tamiya 1/25 scale Ti-

ger I pictured here was the first serious armor model I ever built (and the last full interior!).

The first and most important step in modeling a complete interior is to study every available reference photograph. Examine every detail in every picture and try to figure out what it is, what it does, and what it is attached to. Pay particular attention to electrical cables and details that disappear off one side of a photo; compare photos to see where they reappear, what the whole assembly looks like, and how each item relates to the rest. This detailed research can easily consume several evenings of deep concentration, but the effort will pay off; the more familiar you become with every aspect of the interior, the less likely you'll have to scrape out half the interior and start over again.

Turret detailing. The turret is a good place to start. If you're working with a kit, or if you've cannibalized parts from one, you should have a head start in the form of a simplified gun breech. If not, you'll have to build one from sheet styrene.

When working with a blocky construction like the breech it saves time

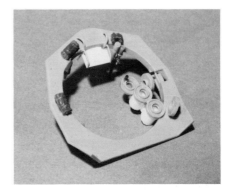

The Pz IVE turret features traversing and elevating gearboxes made from return rollers and Plastruct tube. Viewed through the hatches, these details appear more as vague shapes than identifiable objects.

Steve Zaloga

Steve Zaloga's 1/76 Char B1 bis comes apart to show off its complete interior.

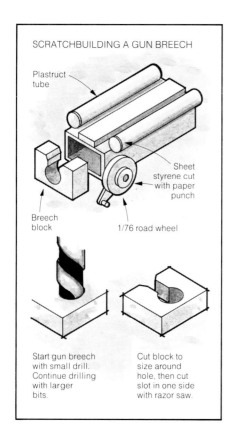

SCRATCHBUILDING A GUN BREECH

Plastruct tube

Sheet styrene cut with paper punch

Breech block

1/76 road wheel

Start gun breech with small drill. Continue drilling with larger bits.

Cut block to size around hole, then cut slot in one side with razor saw.

Jim Stephens' superb 1/25 scale WWI Whippet is one of the finest scratchbuilt armor models I've ever seen. The hull is sheet styrene, detailed with hundreds of Sig copper rivets, and the engine louvers are vacuum-formed. The tracks were cast from a sheet styrene pattern. The roof of the crew compartment is removable to show off the interior.

The gun breech of the Pz IVE. The top half of the breech came from another kit; the rest of the detail is sheet styrene. The spring housing is a Pz IV return roller.

and effort to cut the blocks approximately the right size, assemble, and then sand them down to the final dimensions in place. The trick to drilling the large hole required in the breech is to start with a small drill and use progressively larger sizes until you reach the proper one, then cut out the section at the side of the hole after the drilling operation is finished. If possible, glue a round piece of sprue or tubing into the forward end of the breech assembly to provide a solid connection to the gun mantlet.

When cementing the breech to the mantlet align it carefully, both vertically and horizontally, with the gun barrel. You may have to shim the

More views showing how my Tiger I comes apart. Not the least part of modeling a full interior like this one is the sheer volume

of reference material required. Usually, the details on any given surface had to be pieced together from half a dozen photos.

breech with styrene strips to accomplish this. Detailing the breech is largely a matter of choosing the right material for the right job. Brass or Plastruct tubing can be used for recoil cylinders, and a road wheel makes a good breech block spring housing. Make the pipe frame for the recoil guard and empty casing basket from brass wire with flat styrene panels, then add the appropriate nuts and bolts and bits of plastic.

Next to the gun breech, interior stowage is the most time-consuming aspect of detailing the turret. Closed bins can be made solid, either from laminated styrene sheet or the thicker Evergreen plastic strips, which are ideal. Make open bins from thin styrene sheet, but remember that thin, unsupported sections will gradually warp. It's better to use thicker material — say, .020″ — and bevel the edge where it shows.

An interesting feature of some German tanks, including the Tiger I, was that all equipment on the turret walls was mounted on metal strips secured to the wall at top and bottom. These bands acted as springs, absorbing the shocks of enemy shot hitting the turret and preventing the bins and racks from popping loose and flying around the interior.

Make crew seats and brackets from sheet styrene, Plastruct shapes, and epoxy putty cushions. If the seat goes up and down be sure to include a release handle made from wire or a bit of stretched sprue.

Use your ingenuity for the rest of the turret fittings. Small-scale aircraft landing gear struts make nicely detailed sighting devices, and road wheels from 1/76 armor make excellent traversing and elevating wheels.

Sometimes details come from odd sources: Finding something to represent clear glass vision blocks on my Tiger I presented a problem until I discovered some clear acrylic "ice blocks" in a model railroad shop. The railroad department is also an excellent source for miniature screen, which is intended for use on diesel locomotives.

A detail that usually must be made from scratch and in quantity is German machine gun ammunition bags. These are often found all over the turret and hull, so it's worth your while to make a pattern from epoxy putty and cast duplicates from it.

Detailing the hull. Hull detailing is quite similar to doing the turret, only not quite so complicated. One of the biggest problems is building radios. (Few kits include radios, and those that do never seem to have the right type, or enough of them.) This is time-consuming, but not difficult.

You'll need at least one good photo as reference material. The *German Army Handbook*, published as a field

The Tiger I driver's and radio operator's compartments. Note the ammo stowage.

This German radio bracket has V-shaped rubber shock absorbers on each side.

manual by the U.S. Army during WWII and republished several times since, includes excellent material on German radios. The first thing to remember is that most military radios come as two units, a receiver and a transmitter, so a vehicle will have at least two units. A command vehicle will probably have two units for every frequency being monitored.

Don't let the complex appearance of the radio scare you. Each knob and dial is easy to make — there are just a lot of them. Make a styrene box and detail it with bits of styrene sheet and sprue in accordance with your reference photos. Build the mounting frame around the radios from Plastruct and sheet styrene.

Next to the radios, the most difficult hull details to make are the seats, which usually require tubular frame construction. Make the frames from brass wire, and if you need two or more the same size, bend the frames around a block of wood carved to the right shape.

German vehicles used zigzag wire springs, which can also be made from brass wire. You'll probably need a lot of these, so it's worth making a simple jig to bend the wire. While the springs can be installed before the epoxy putty seat cushions, it's easier to install the springs afterwards, so the cushion provides something solid to glue to.

To make the safety tread on the hull and turret floor, take a piece of fine-mesh wire screen and rub a piece of heavy-duty aluminum foil down onto it with a pencil eraser. The result will be a perfect tread pattern on the foil, which can then be glued to the styrene floor.

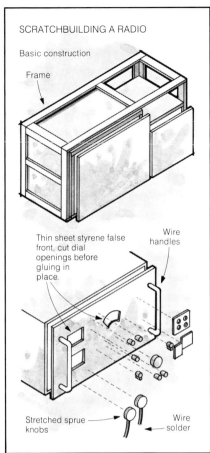

SCRATCHBUILDING A RADIO

Basic construction

Frame

Thin sheet styrene false front, cut dial openings before gluing in place.

Wire handles

Stretched sprue knobs

Wire solder

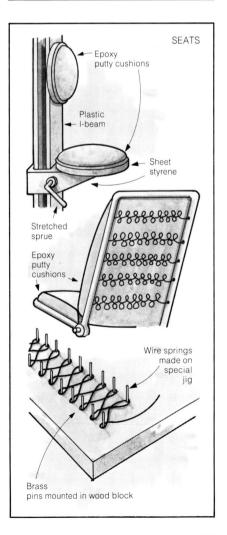

SEATS

Epoxy putty cushions

Plastic I-beam

Sheet styrene

Stretched sprue

Epoxy putty cushions

Wire springs made on special jig

Brass pins mounted in wood block

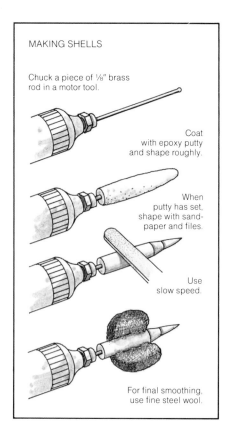

MAKING SHELLS

Chuck a piece of ⅛" brass rod in a motor tool.

Coat with epoxy putty and shape roughly.

When putty has set, shape with sandpaper and files.

Use slow speed.

For final smoothing, use fine steel wool.

Transmissions are easy to build. Make a "Dagwood" sandwich of various sizes of road wheels from kits, and if the transmission should include a tapered section, try using the cone-shaped section from a German drive sprocket.

Instrument panels can be salvaged from aircraft, car, or truck kits, particularly 1/32 or 1/24 scale. If you don't want to ruin the kit part, just make an RTV mold of the panel, then cast it as described in Chapter 5. Additional dials for instrument panels can be found in the radio control department of your hobby shop.

Jim Stephens has developed an interesting technique for casting flat parts such as instrument panels. He rubs a piece of aluminum foil down snugly onto the original piece, then carefully peels it off. Next he fills the cavity with scraps of plastic sprue and puts it in a hot oven (about 400°) for about 15 minutes, until the plastic melts. After allowing the plastic to cool he peels off the foil, leaving an acceptable duplicate of the original part.

Much of the hull is taken up with ammunition storage, with bins under the floor and on the sides near the driver and radio operator. These bins are easy to build from sheet styrene, and it's a nice touch to model one of them open, with several shells exposed. If you can find the right size shells in a kit you're all set; otherwise, you'll have to turn your own.

You don't need a lathe. Chuck a piece of ⅛" brass rod in a motor tool, leaving the length of the shell plus about ¼" projecting from the collet. Cover the rod with epoxy putty and rough out the shell — you can even run the tool on low speed and work the putty like clay on a potter's wheel, but don't try for much more than an approximate shape. After the putty has set, run the motor tool at medium speed and use sandpaper and files for final shaping. Once you've made an accurate master, cast as many additional shells as you need.

Detailing engine compartments. The engine compartment of a tank contains a lot of machinery, so don't start entirely from scratch unless you absolutely have to. A car or truck kit should yield an engine block approxi-mately the right size and configuration, as well as air filters, carburetors, distributors, and other useful details. Also check 1/32 and 1/24 aircraft kits for in-line engines (or a radial engine, if you're detailing a Sherman). Once you have the block, assembling a convincing engine is largely a matter of adding bits of styrene sheet, sprue, wire solder, and assorted cut-up model railroad parts.

Engine detailing involves a technique I call "creative gizmology": the use of bits and pieces scrounged from anywhere and everywhere to simulate complex machinery that would be exhausting to make any other way. The most famous examples of this were the spacecraft created for such films as *2001: A Space Odyssey* and *Star Wars*. These models were detailed with hundreds of parts scavenged from kits. The major difference between the space modelers and us armor modelers is that while they can design the machinery to suit the available parts, we have to duplicate real-world machines with whatever gizmos we can find.

The best source for gizmos is the railroad department of your hobby shop. Cal-Scale, Grandt Line, and several other firms offer brass and plastic detail parts for O and HO scale railroad cars and locomotives, and although the brass parts are expensive if you need them in quantity, the plastic ones are cheap and the detail is simply amazing.

You will not want to use unmodified railroad parts often (they soon become recognizable even to fellow armor modelers), but you can cut them apart and recombine them to your heart's content. This is the basic idea behind gizmology, which, from a purely practical standpoint, yields 90 percent of the results of painstakingly accurate modeling in only 10 percent of the time.

Gizmology is not, however, a license to conjure up whole mechanisms out of thin air. The idea is to use available parts to represent mechanisms that actually existed, not to create new ones of your own. Always work from photographs of the real thing, and take the time to duplicate them as closely as possible.

Besides the engine itself, engine compartments also contain fuel tanks, air intake and exhaust fans, and cooling systems. Radiators can be cannibalized from car kits or model railroad parts, and the same is true of fans (in desperation I once used an HO scale wagon wheel for a fan, and it worked fine). Fuel tanks usually have square corners, but some are odd-shaped to conform to the available space in the vehicle. They can easily be built up from sheet styrene and sanded to final shape. Don't forget to include the fuel lines that lead to the engine.

George Woodard

The fully detailed engine compartment of George Woodard's prizewinning Duster. George was lucky (or unlucky, depending upon how you look at it!) that the entire back end of the vehicle could be opened up like this to show off his handiwork.

An M25 tank transporter

The M25 tank transporter was one of the most unusual vehicles used by the U. S. Army in World War II. Consisting of an M26 tractor and an M15 trailer, it featured an armored cab for recovering damaged tanks under fire, and chain drive, which had long since been abandoned for most trucks this size.

The M25 saw limited service in Europe in 1944-45. The Allied advance across France was so swift that recovery under fire was not often necessary, and late-production M26s had plain sheet metal cabs, a weight-saving measure which improved the performance of the underpowered tractor.

This 1/35 scale model was built, like the Israeli Super Sherman in Chapter 9, for the "Road to Damascus" diorama in my earlier book, HOW TO BUILD DIORAMAS. I started with the Max kit — in spite of warnings from experienced modelers that it left a great deal to be desired. Cocksure, I looked over all the parts in the box (and the box art, which was terrific) and figured that all the model needed was a little extra detailing.

Was I ever wrong! Not only were entire assemblies on the real thing missing from the kit, but others had been devised entirely from the kit designers' imaginations. The wheels were almost pitifully small, and many other dimensions were off as well.

In the end, the only salvageable parts proved to be the cab and frame, both of which had to be extensively modified. Even so, the cab is not quite the right shape, and if I had to do it over again I'd build it, too, from scratch. Still, I had gotten it into my head that I wanted a tank transporter in the scene, and I was determined to have one (at any cost, as it turned out!). This chapter shows how it was done, and includes accurate working drawings should you wish to try your hand at a similar model. It's an exercise in all the scratchbuilding and detailing techniques discussed in earlier chapters.

The transporter during field trials. This shows the basic configuration of tractor and trailer. The trailer on my model differs slightly; it is the M15A2, which was widened and strengthened to accommodate the larger M26 Pershing tank. The wheel ramps of the later version were also modified.

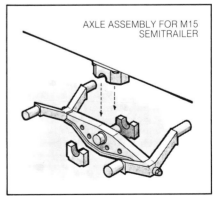

AXLE ASSEMBLY FOR M15 SEMITRAILER

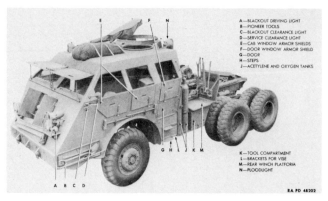

A—BLACKOUT DRIVING LIGHT
B—PIONEER TOOLS
C—BLACKOUT CLEARANCE LIGHT
D—SERVICE CLEARANCE LIGHT
E—CAB WINDOW ARMOR SHIELDS
F—DOOR WINDOW ARMOR SHIELD
G—DOOR
H—STEPS
J—ACETYLENE AND OXYGEN TANKS

K—TOOL COMPARTMENT
L—BRACKETS FOR VISE
M—REAR WINCH PLATFORM
N—FLOODLIGHT

RA PD 48202

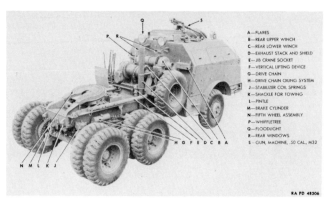

A—FLARES
B—REAR UPPER WINCH
C—REAR LOWER WINCH
D—EXHAUST STACK AND SHIELD
E—JIB CRANE SOCKET
F—VERTICAL LIFTING DEVICE
G—DRIVE CHAIN
H—DRIVE CHAIN OILING SYSTEM
J—STABILIZER COIL SPRINGS
K—SHACKLE FOR TOWING
L—PINTLE
M—BRAKE CYLINDER
N—FIFTH WHEEL ASSEMBLY
P—WHIFFLETREE
Q—FLOODLIGHT
R—REAR WINDOWS
S—GUN, MACHINE, .50 CAL, M32

RA PD 48206

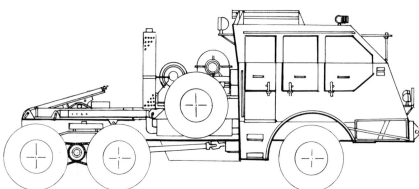

My primary reference was a copy of War Department Technical Manual TM 9-767, which contained hundreds of photos, including these overall views. Using the photos and specifications I made the working drawings that are reproduced here in 1/70 scale. To enlarge these plans to 1/35 scale take the book to a photostat or blueprint shop and ask for a 200 percent enlargement.

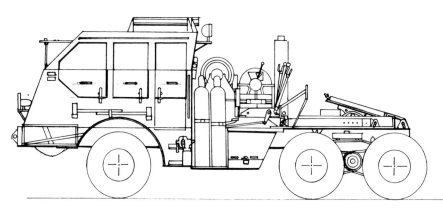

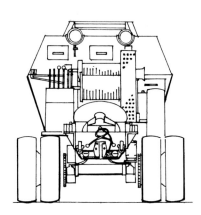

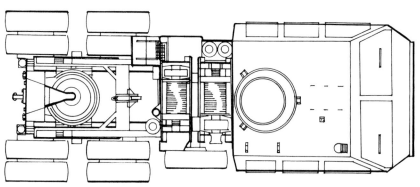

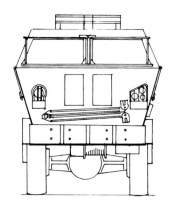

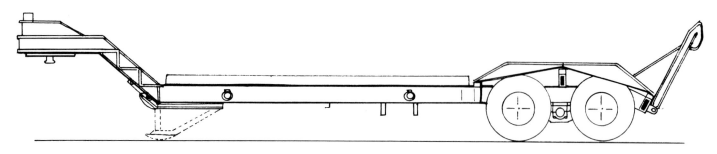

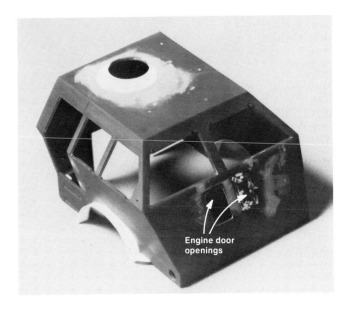

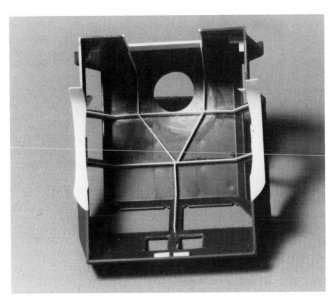

Engine door openings

Reworking the cab included plugging the top hatch with sheet styrene and cutting a new opening in the correct position. (Left) At this point the engine door opening on the right had been roughed out with a motor tool and saw, while the other had already been trimmed to final shape. (Right) The cab interior bracing is made from .020″ styrene, ⅛″ wide.

(Left) Modifications to the cab floor included deepening the wheel wells, covering the unsightly hinges on the original, and adding an .020″ strip on each side to correct a loose fit. I also added a radiator front made from aluminum model railroad screen and an engine compartment.

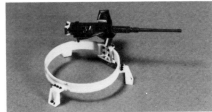

(Above) The ring mount for the roof was heat-formed around a brass tube and detailed as described in Chapter 7.

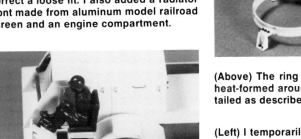

(Left) I temporarily glued the driver to his seat to make sure it was the right height. Here, his feet don't touch the pedals, but that was corrected later. The engine compartment access doors are of .010″ styrene with brass wire hooks and handles.

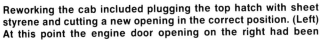

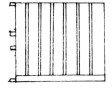

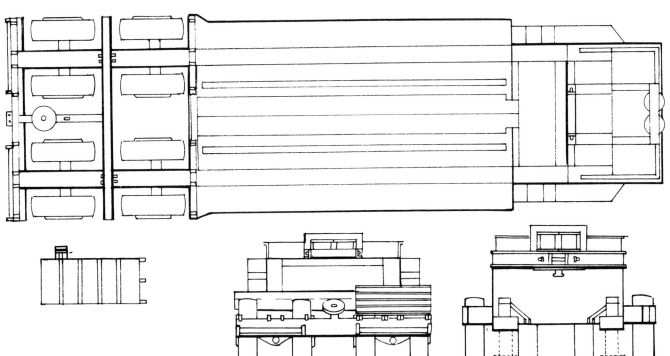

(Above) I used wheels scavenged from the Adams/SNAP/Lifelike atomic cannon kit. The kit provided only 10 of the 19 required for the transporter, so I cast the rest. This wheel from a Monogram M8 armored car is also about the right size, but had to be widened with a sandwich of three sheets of .040″ styrene, cut to approximate shape and trimmed after assembly. Laminating 19 tires like this would be a real job, so you'd do better to make one or two and cast the rest.

The underside of the model shows a lot of white plastic in evidence. The axle and transfer case are from a Monogram M8 armored car, although if I built the model again (not a chance!) I would use parts from a truck kit. Notice the Plastruct tube extenders to lengthen the axle and the styrene risers added under the springs.

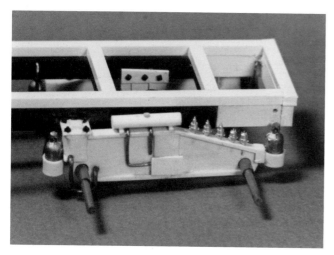

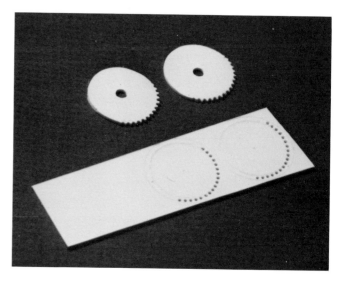

The completed rear axle frames, glued to the frame, with brass wire axles poking through. The air reservoir at each end of the frame is the breech end of a Dahlgren gun from a model ship kit, cut off and wrapped in sheet styrene; the five oil fittings on the sloped portion of the frame are Cal-Scale brass HO model railroad pop valves; and the numerous nuts and bolts are Grandt Line parts.

(Above and below) The sprockets were made as described in Chapter 11, and the drive chain from a Monogram 1/25 Mack truck was carefully wrapped around them. Note the styrene strips added to correct the thickness of the vehicle frame.

The power train, showing the main gearbox (which had a power takeoff for the winches above it), and the drive-shafts and U-joints to the front and rear axles. Most of the drive train elements are from a Monogram armored car.

The vertical lifting frame in its upright position. It was normally stowed in the collapsed position on the vehicle frame.

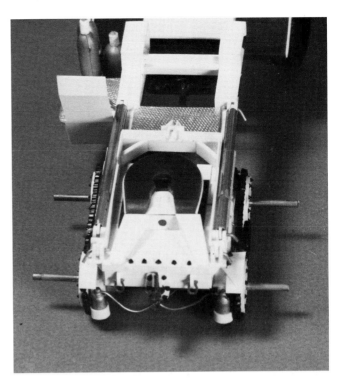

(Right) The rear of the tractor, showing the vertical lifting frame on the model before installation of the winches. The "fifth wheel" (the platform on which the trailer rests and pivots) was taken from the Max kit, with added detail. Note the styrene ramps leading to the fifth wheel, the tow pintle scavenged from the Monogram armored car, and the other fittings on the back plate. The safety tread was made from aluminum foil, and each of the welding bottles was made from two 1/48 airplane bombs with a cap made of Plastruct tubing.

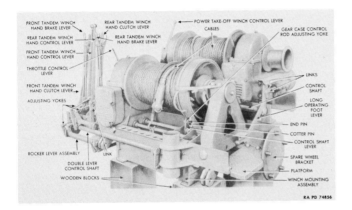

A good tech manual view of the winches, the most complicated subassembly on the model. The winches themselves are identical, but placed in opposite directions on the frame. The barely visible winch under the cab is also similar.

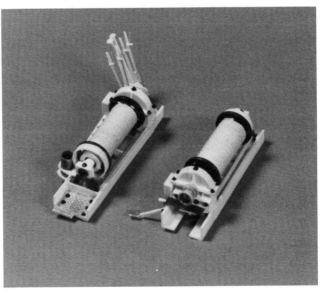

The completed winches. The cable reel was adapted from the telephone reels in the Tamiya Jeep kit, widened with Plastruct tube; the rest was built from sheet styrene and stretched sprue.

Two views of the completed tractor. Virtually anything white is straightforward sheet styrene construction. The perforated exhaust guard is aluminum hi-fi speaker screen, carefully bent around a dowel. The searchlights on the back of the cab were scavenged from a truck kit. The wedge-shaped device behind the left side of the cab is a towing frame called a "whiffletree."

(Above) After the extensive work required on the tractor the trailer was a breeze, because most of the construction was straight sheet styrene. The basic frame of the trailer was used as provided in the kit, since I did not have enough reference on the M15A1 trailer to rework it with much confidence. The rear end of the completed model shows the loading ramps, their wire supports, and my home-cast wheels.

(Above and right) Close-ups of the finished model. Note the profusion of chocks, chains, ropes, toolboxes, and other rigging gear on the front deck of the trailer.

The completed transporter with the Israeli Super Sherman (Chapter 9) aboard. Even unpainted, with all the white plastic showing the M25 and its load make a very impressive model — not to mention their size!